Reflections On Old Age

Reflections On Old Age
A Study in Christian Humanism

Cornelius F. Murphy Jr.

RESOURCE *Publications* • Eugene, Oregon

REFLECTIONS ON OLD AGE
A Study in Christian Humanism

Copyright © 2015 Cornelius F. Murphy Jr. All rights reserved. Except for brief quotations in critical publications or reviews, no part of this book may be reproduced in any manner without prior written permission from the publisher. Write: Permissions. Wipf and Stock Publishers, 199 W. 8th Ave., Suite 3, Eugene, OR 97401.

Resource Publications
An Imprint of Wipf and Stock Publishers
199 W. 8th Ave., Suite 3
Eugene, OR 97401

www.wipfandstock.com

ISBN 13: 978-1-4982-1885-6

Manufactured in the U.S.A.   04/06/2015

This book is dedicated to the Administrators, employees, and residents of St. Barnabas Communities who, with great care and kindness, have eased my transition into this penultimate stage of life.

Contents

Preface | ix

1. Old Age Through The Ages | 1
2. Longevity and the Sciences of Aging | 31
3. The Quest For Maturity | 58
4. Last Things | 87

Bibliography | 115
Index | 119

Preface

SINCE THE DAWN OF the last century we have experienced a significant increase in life expectancy. From an average age of about fifty in 1900 many now can expect to live well into their eighties. But as the numbers of older persons increases, their position in society continues to decline. For the young, as well as for those in their prime, the aged part of the population is generally out of sight as well as out of mind. To counter that marginalization, we must first have a greater understanding of how the elderly have been thought of throughout the history of our Western civilization. That is the focus of the first chapter, *Old Age Through The Ages*. It begins with the situation in Ancient Greece and Rome and concludes with the circumstances of the elderly at the close of the nineteenth century.

To Plato, the human being was assumed to be a composite of both body and soul, and that premise guided his appraisal of old age as well as his general philosophy. He and other thinkers of that period took note of the distortions of character and bodily decay that accompany old age, but they also believed that this advanced stage of life provided opportunities for immaterial pleasures which were earlier ignored or underdeveloped. They were sure that intellectual comprehension could be improved, and that as we grow older we can enjoy modes of conviviality that are not spoiled by pride or rivalry. It was generally agreed that as we grow older we begin to live more deeply within ourselves. The classic *De Senectute* by Cicero reaffirmed and expanded upon these ideas.

For the philosophers and poets of the ancient world personal character was the unchangeable result of what had been done before an individual reached old age. In the medieval period, however, Christian ideals began to influence the general culture and spiritual improvement became an ideal that affected every stage of life. Dante had important insights into the possibilities of growth in the later years, which, as we shall see, have a relevance to our own time. He believed that moral development was well within the capacities of older persons, especially since their experiences had given them a deeper understanding of the principles of justice and the value of compassion. Dante thought that those of advanced years had a magnanimity that could be of great benefit to the community at large.

In the late Middle Ages affirmative appraisals of old age were in competition with more morbid images of decline. Both Chaucer and Shakespeare had dim views of the later years. But a more profound pessimism flowed from the pen of the French writer Michel de Montaigne. He thought that by the age of twenty the human soul is as fully developed, as it will ever be. Moreover, he thought that the continued employment of older men was unjust because it reduced the opportunities for the young. In subsequent centuries industrialization and compulsory retirement would make his ideas matters of public policy.

With the coming of the modern age some creative writers challenged Montaigne's principles. The great German humanist Goethe wrote the final part of his *Faust* when he was in his eighties. In England, Samuel Johnson took up the problem of intergenerational relations, even though he thought there was little chance of reconciling " the contraries of Spring and Winter". There were some positive models for aging in the lives of public figures such as in the long tenure of Queen Victoria and the political career of the statesman Gladstone. Poetic appraisals were mixed: Browning and Tennyson offer comforting images; there were dour assessments of old age in the poetry of Matthew Arnold.

As the isolation of older men and women from their families increased, institutional care came into favor. But the results were not encouraging. Those among the elderly who were receiving public assistance tended to narrow their range of interests, lose all vitality, and become extremely self-centered. Some of the best writers of the Victorian age saw how demeaning was the general situation and they made imaginative appeals to draw older men

Preface

and women into closer association with the rest of the community. The calls for a more inclusive society were usually ignored, but they had the value of raising for us the issue of what *place* an older person should have in society at large as well as pointing to the possibilities of intergenerational communication.

In a final section of the opening chapter I examine the circumstances of the elderly in America from the colonial times to the period following the Civil War. At the beginning, the elderly constituted only about two percent of the population, yet their needs and circumstances were given considerable attention. Puritan sermons drew heavily upon Old Testament descriptions of the values of old age, but deeper tensions were developing between the generations. The elderly had disproportionate economic resources, particularly with respect to land, and this situation caused considerable resentment. These problems intensified after the American Revolution because principles of Equality called into questions all distinctions of rank and privilege.

Fortunately, in the course of time, there was a New England Renaissance of arts and letters that took a more positive position on the values of old age. Ralph Waldo Emerson had read Cicero's classic and made a forceful restatement of the great Roman's optimistic understanding of advanced life. Emerson thought that without the influence of the old there could be no true civilization. Oliver Wendell Holmes, a man of letters as well as a medical practitioner, believed that at every stage of life there were oscillations between immaturity and complete development, and that older persons would approach their own perfection so long as they did not allow the routine of habitual practices to interfere with the powers of self-development.

As the nineteenth century was drawing to a close, improvements in industrial production and the expansion of the commercial culture were developing in a manner that excluded older persons –even as their life expectancies were increasing. Seen as impediments to progress, the old were treated with remorseless indifference. In the coming century, advances in science and medicine would improve the physical prospects of old age but do little to relieve the sense of social abandonment. The second chapter explores how reflective thought would be compelled to address the problematic aspects of human longevity.

Scientists working at the beginning of the twentieth century took note of the differences between humans and other animal species. In the sub-human, the time between reproduction and death was short, while human beings have the possibility of living for a considerable period of time after they have brought new life into the world. Many began to believe that science and technology could indefinitely expand the period of human life, and during the presidency of George W. Bush a commission was established to examine, among other things, the social desirability of such an ambition. This distinguished Council on Bioethics paid particular attention to the scientific discoveries that were meant not only to conquer existing diseases of the elderly but also to increase both the average and maximum life span. In this chapter I examine the report of the Council *Beyond Therapy: Biotechnology and The Pursuit of Happiness (2003)* and discuss its reservation concerning the desire to infinitely expand human life.

Substantial improvements in the physical health of human beings is clearly on the rise, but we would do well not to believe that "to breathe were life." The present danger is that otherwise healthy older individuals are simply marking time or allowing their extended life to be one of monotonous duration. Every older person undoubtedly declines, but he or she should also move into a fuller stage of growth and maturity. In terms of prevailing metaphors, the elderly should not treat the extension of life as an anchorage, but rather as a new landfall where they can go forward, in trust, into an unknown future. But that healthy objective is impeded by the increase in their social isolation. Too often, those of advanced years are like Lear: unaccomodated by their families and having no meaningful role in the ongoing life of society at large.

One remedy for this unworthy situation is to promote the reconciliation of the generations. The ideal is to create a society that is welcoming to all persons at every stage in the development of human life. When properly instructed, the young can come to see

PREFACE

the advantages of contact with the experience and wisdom of the elderly; conversely, older persons must not only give the young encouragement, but also be willing to accept whatever redistribution of social and economic resources that are needed so that younger persons have a reasonable chance to develop their prospects in life.

Reconciliation must extend across the whole range of generations. Justified attention is given to the relationships between the old and the young, but we must also bring the elderly and those of middle age closer together. Older persons need to initiate conversations with all those younger than themselves about the quality of life in this technologically derived, consumerist society. Here the wisdom of age becomes of critical importance, because it is only after extensive experience that a person fully understands how much of the culture that most take for granted is in reality unjust and inhuman. And those now profiting from the expansive materialism need to develop the humility needed to listen to those older than themselves about what in our culture should be corrected as well as that which deserves to be affirmed. It is within this framework that the great issues of stability and change can be meaningfully addressed.

In a final section of this second chapter I consider the plight of the very old—those over eighty-five, mostly women, and mostly institutionalized, who experience the most severe suffering and isolation. Many wonder if living so long can be squared with the hope of living well. These persons need to be convinced that their continued existence makes a meaningful difference in the lives of others. Their plight raises importance issues about the allocation of social resources, but it also brings out the importance of Martin Buber's dictum that to be alive is to be spoken to.

In the third chapter, entitled *The Quest For Maturity* we approach the difficulties of establishing a personal identity after passing into old age. As the conventional and professional sources of self-esteem fall away the challenge is to discover who we are within ourselves. The hope is that we shall discover something of real substance. Building ourselves up from within, we begin to live more in harmony with our circumstances and develop the virtues and experience the pleasures that are essential to the full extension of life. Some will try to find themselves through volunteering, which is of great value, but we are more likely to plumb the depths of our being by reflection than by action.

From the time of Cicero those who have thought seriously about the meaning of old age have looked upon it as a time for the flowering of intellect and intuition. Relieved of the pressures of the work–a–day world, older persons can bring out inner powers that are no longer subject to pragmatic purposes. They can begin to see the value of whatever is true, good, or beautiful as it is in itself. Contemplation can fill the space made vacant by the loss of work, but it is difficult for one no longer employed to make proper use of the now available time. Here the temperance so important to physical health becomes applicable to the well being of the total personality.

A proper use of leisure provides an opening to the world of knowledge in all its dimensions. Under the circumstances of modern life, however, one who desires to enrich his heart and mind must abstain from much of which constitutes popular culture. This forbearance must be balanced by the deliberate pursuit of books, programs, music, and other materials that can elevate the understanding and expand the feelings of an elderly person.

Thoughtfulness originates in solitude but it has social implications. As the mind deepens, so does the desire to share what is learned with others. And this can be done in public venues as well as under circumstances of more intimate discussion. Throughout the country 'Conversation Salons' are being made available in public libraries to give citizens opportunities to discuss public issues under conditions of civility. Seniors have much to contribute to these exchanges. Old age has brought a release from passion that applies to matters political as well as those of sexuality. Older individuals engaged in open dialogue should be free from the rancor of division that have poisoned our politics and have a conciliatory influence upon the discussions. An older generation should manifest a collective wisdom.

Those who are of an advanced age can have a constructive public influence without holding public office. Much depends upon how much they care about the common good. To have such an inclusive moral vision they must first free themselves from the vices that traditionally have haunted old age. These means overcoming their own narrowness, their self-absorption, and any willful isolation from the world around them. They need to think forward, not just remember the past. Through such corrections, older persons can show that a civilized existence can still come into being.

As citizens, older persons can be brought into collaborative discussion with others over what constitutes the common good. These dialogues are civil but not intimate. The greater part of the relatedness that makes up our final years are with others with whom we are more closely connected. The quality of those relationships has an important bearing upon our prospects for a long life. Those who are married have the greatest intimacies, even if they are more spiritual than sexual in nature. The relationship that older persons have with children and other relatives is more problematic. Such difficulties can be a matter of a particular family history, but it also has to do with the age segregation that has become so much a part of modern life. Each individual shares the interests of his own age group and cares little about those at a different stage of life.

Even when relations within families are warm and amiable, they should not be exclusive. Associations outside the home are valuable at every stage of life. In old age women are still drawn to the company of other women, especially if they are widows. For older men to enjoy the company of other men is more complicated because the sense of personal independence is stronger. Older men seem to prefer general gatherings to separate encounters, but they should not ignore the advantages of genuine friendship. To have a friend is liberating because, as Emerson observed, with a friend one is free to think aloud. And, in charity, one should exhibit a real friendliness towards anyone who is alone and feels isolated from the rest of the community.

The various forms of relatedness, both public and private that occur in old age take us to the farthest limits of the horizontal dimensions of our lives. At the same time, we gradually become more aware of the vertical dimensions of human existence. With death always nearer, we realize, more fully than at any other time in life our ultimate dependence upon the mercies of Divine Providence. This can lead us to attend more carefully to prayer and the ceremonies of worship, but we also begin to think about the relationship between this world and the next. Thus it is appropriate that we shall close these reflections with a final chapter on *Ultimate Things*.

What does it mean to be a complete human being? The answer of the secular world is that all our expectations for happiness are confined to the experiences of life on earth, which is autonomous and self-sufficient. Death is not to be feared because it brings simple extinction. To deal with such positions it is well that these reflections have a strong historical quality. For Cicero was aware of the possibilities of extinction but in his classic treatise *On Old Age* (De *Senectute*) he preferred to think of the alternative: the passage of the soul to some place where it shall live forever and find a reunion with those whom in this life he had loved or admired.

Something similar to Cicero's view can be found in a Symposium published in 1910 entitled *In After Days: Thoughts on the Future Life*. Literary celebrities of the time, such as William Dean Howells, Julia Ward Howe, and Henry James, as well as lesser-known writers, all made contributions. Many, like Cicero, expressed a hope for reunion with loved ones and the general belief was in a merciful rather than a vindictive Deity. There was also a strong passion for immortality; a belief in the continuance and full development of the individual personality. The contribution of Henry James, under the provocative title *"Is There Life After Death?"* raised the most interesting issues. James equated personality with consciousness and for him the artistic form of awareness was of basic importance. Its development leads to a hope for a greater satisfaction beyond the grave.

The anticipation of some form of afterlife is too deeply a part of human history to be ignored, and whatever its character it has usually been thought of as having to do with rewards, or punishments. I turn James' concentration upon the centrality of artistic consciousness to an emphasis upon moral conscience for it is here that the dramatic struggle between good and evil occurs. And I also point out how from both classical and biblical traditions comes the belief that accountability at death, of our righteousness or our wrongdoing, is what determines the final destiny of the human person.

Throughout the centuries, those who have written about old age have expressed the belief that the nearness of death entails proximity of judgment. Powerful images of the Last Judgment in the Book of Revelation and in the artistic creations of medieval Europe caused great anxiety among believers, as did the doctrine of Predestination taught by the Calvinists. In this age such distress has largely disappeared either because of the spread of disbelief or because of a growing emphasis upon the unlimited range of Divine Mercy. While this is much to the good, it can lead to a facile assumption of salvation and a hasty conclusion about the eternal prospects of others.

Another misconception is the belief that the passage into eternity is that of an immaterial soul finally relieved of the burden of a body. This attitude appears in Cicero and even into the 1910 Symposium. But for Christians, a belief in personal immortality is a conviction that eternal life is an extension to human beings of the Resurrection of Jesus Christ from the dead. In conformity with that event, at the Last Judgment there shall be a revival of the whole human person, body and soul, as well as a final accounting of the whole of human history.

Faith in a Last Judgment is not easy to contemplate. But it gives all who suffer injustice an expectation that God will, in His time, bring his vindication in a complete undoing of all wrong. But if the end were only one of absolute justice it would be fearful for all. Our understanding of eternity must be one of forgiveness as well. Our hope must be for an eternity where we will be with all who died in God's love and where the fullness of His peace will reign forever. It will be a supreme satisfaction both for the individual person and for the whole community of the redeemed, for there will be a banquet of unity in which all have been built up into a dwelling place for God.

1

Old Age Through the Ages

The Ancient World

SEVERAL YEARS AGO I visited Beijing and there I had the opportunity for a conversation with a Chinese philosopher. We discussed, amicably, the differences between our political and economic systems and found some point of agreement on certain issues. But at the end he said: "There is one thing in your culture with which we can never imitate: your worship of the young". And one of the distinguishing features of Chinese civilization is their Confucian ethic that demands deference to the elderly. Here in the West, our attitude towards old age has been more various and complicated. The best way to approach the subject is to review some of the major themes that have developed over the course of the history of our civilization. Let us begin with looking at the situation in Ancient Greece.

In his famous book *The Republic* the philosopher Plato affirmed the importance of old age. He stood against those who grumbled and whined about the condition, or were always feeling sorry for themselves, emphasizing the physical pains and social isolation that they experienced. To Plato, the complainers had always been dissatisfied with their circumstances at every stage of life, while those who have a warm and happy character hardly feel the difficulties of growing old. And old age had its advantages. When passions release their hold, we have escaped not from one master but from many. Moreover, as the pleasures of the body fade, more spiritual enjoyments, such as those of thought and unhurried conversation increase. Cephalus, who appears as a character at the beginning of the book, is a patriarch who serves as a model for an old man nearing the end of his life. He is at peace with himself and with all mankind. While recognizing the importance of adequate resources, he is generally indifferent to riches. For him, moderate enjoyment makes old age a tolerable phase of human existence. Cephalus is able to raise important questions, such as those concerning justice, but he soon departs from the dialogues.

As explained in *The Republic,* advanced age was also a time for private reflection; especially concerning the anticipation of future rewards and punishments. As death nears, fears of afterlife increase. Plato advises those who earlier in life had done wrong to reform and repent. All who are aging should live out the remainder of their lives justly, avoiding extremes of conduct so that hope can be the 'nurse' of their final years.

There was also a political significance to old age. In an ideal community, philosophers would be kings, and since growth of reflection takes time to develop, some of the elderly would have opportunities to govern.[1]

Aristotle, the other great Greek philosopher, thought that the elderly should be consulted, but not rule, in matters of politics. He also compared the character of the aged with the qualities of youth. [2]Aristotle noted that the young spend their lives in expectation rather than in memory, and that they are governed more by moral feeling than by reasoning. They also have strong passions and are anxious to show their superiority. The young are also fonder of their friends and they trust others readily because they have not yet been cheated. They love and hate too much. On the other hand, those who are past their prime neither love warmly nor hate bitterly. And the elderly, having been humbled by life, have few grand expectations.[3]

Aristotle also had a dim view of the character of those who are elderly. He thought that they are overly fond of themselves and

1. *The Republic* Part One ch.1; Part III.
2. *The Rhetoric* Bk.II, ch. 12–13.
3. Ibid.

that they prefer what is useful to what is noble. Like the late Andy Rooney, those who are advanced in years are not too concerned about what other people may think of them. With age, the virtue of frugality becomes the vice of stinginess. The elderly are not generous because they know too well that money is hard to come by and even harder to keep. Moreover, they lack confidence in a future. They are always anticipating disappointments and they lack the courage needed to face what is uncertain and precarious.

If we move from Greece to Rome we find reflections that both stressed the sadness of old age and its positive opportunities. In his famous Ode 2.14 the poet Horace warned that wrinkles cannot be delayed by devotion, nor can the assault of old age and death be delayed. All must face "the gloomy stream which must be crossed by all of us who feed on the bounty of earth". Dramatists mocked the aged and sought to undermine the authority of the *paterfamilias* that invested power over domestic society in the eldest male. Cruelest of all was the Roman satirical poet, Juvenal, (c.60-140) who, with great descriptive power, detailed the physical flaws of the elderly. Thus, in contrast to the young, whose vigor was various, "the old are all alike, and they look it . . . a disgusting sight to themselves, their wives, and their children."[4]

By contrast, Cicero, the greatest lawyer politician, philosopher and literary genius of his time, expressed an optimistic view in his classic treatise *On Old Age (De Senectute)* that was written in 44 B C. Cicero was a stoic. He believed that the best life was one lived according to reason. By that standard; he thought old age had many advantages. In his classic essay he dealt with several charges against old age. The first was that it withdraws us from the active life. To this Cicero responded that the objection assumes that only those who are young and strong can do useful work. But there are many occupations fitted for the talents and brains of the old, even if they may be physically feeble. He pointed to those in the history of Rome who used the experience and authority of their advanced years for the common weal. And then there was the wonderful example he uses of the pilot of a ship. The one at the rudder may

4. Horace, Ode 2.4; Juvenal, Satire x.

not be running around and hauling sail like the younger crew, but his task is of greater importance because all depend upon his guidance. "Great deeds" wrote Cicero, "are not done by strength, or speed, or physique; they are the products of thought and character and judgment. And far from diminishing, such qualities actually increase with age."[5]

Increasing age also brings about a decline of physical strength. Surely that makes old age objectionable! Not really, according to Cicero. Such decline is devastating only for those who were foolish enough to trust in their muscles to make their way in life. Besides, the course of nature is such that, if we have lived a virtuous life, we should have enough physical strength left to meet most of the demands of growing old.

An even stronger objection to old age was that it necessarily leads to a decrease in sensual pleasure. Like Plato, Cicero believed that a release from the passions brought a certain moral freedom. Cicero was a bit of a Puritan. He was convinced that whenever lustful desires abounded, a good life measured by reason was impossible. As for pleasures of the palate, they were legitimate, in moderation, throughout life. But in old age a meal among friends is not just an occasion for satisfying an appetite. Nor was it an end in itself. Such a meeting was a *convivium,* a coming together in which company and conversation gradually take precedence over gastronomic delights.

Another objection raises an issue that today is very delicate: the loss of memory in old age. Cicero's manner of dealing with the problem may be considered insensitive, at least insofar as he believed the decline is due either to a lack of native intelligence, or to a failure to generously use the powers of thinking and reflection with which we are endowed. But there is some truth in his idea that the old can always remember whatever is of interest to them.

For a culture such as ours, that places such hopes in youthful initiative, the values of athleticism, and a hedonistic life-style, Cicero's philosophy may seem truly antique. But there is much enduring wisdom in his thinking. For when the attractions of sex,

---

5. *On Old Age* I., VI.

ambition, and rivalry are gone, it is important that those who are growing old retain a belief that, in spite of the increase in years, they may still have a meaningful life. The gain can be one of a clarified self-understanding and confidence, so long as the aging individual does not let external circumstances determine his destiny.

Cicero believed that old age was the time when a person begins to live within himself. Over time, one becomes aware of inward powers that, though less consciously deployed in earlier states of life, can bring much happiness to the advancing years. Of all the advantages, of primary importance were the powers of intellect within those who are sensible and who are well enough educated to understand the inherent value of the mind. Those growing old should continue to gain in knowledge, not only of themselves, but also of the broader world of which they are a part. If they do so, they will experience some of the greatest pleasure of age. This is an insight of perennial value.[6]

To the objection that old are unhappy because they are socially isolated, Cicero retorts that if their lives are lively and not sluggish, others will desire to be in their company. Intergenerational contact is especially important. The old should prefer the company of promising youth, and the young hoping to mature should welcome the advice of their elders because it can help them develop a good life for themselves.

An increase in aesthetic enjoyments can moderate a sense of isolation. Cicero appreciated the values and the pleasures of the rural life, which had given him "an unbelievable amount of enjoyment." Planting and cultivating leads to the contemplation of the beauty and order that lie within the processes of nature as a whole. According to this Roman philosopher, no life could be happier than that of a farmer.

Of all the advantages of growing old, receiving respect is the greatest glory. Cicero is careful to note that veneration must be earned. Esteem is the culmination of a life well spent; especially when a man who has grown old has had a distinguished career.

---

6. Ibid., I. VII.

As for the faults of the old, as described by Aristotle—ill-temper, mean spiritedness, and the like—these, to Cicero, are faults of character, not of age.

In *De Senectute* there are some important thoughts on the nearness of death, which is the final objection to the process of growing old. Cicero thought that he understood what mortality means. Believing that our souls are implanted by heaven into our bodies, he accepts the Socratic teaching on its immateriality and immortality. Cicero finds the arguments intellectually persuasive but he also has some empirical evidence. He observes that the wise die with the greatest equanimity, which implies that they have some knowledge that they are on their way to a better world. As a philosopher, he intuits the course of nature and knows that it has granted us life on earth as a temporary home. As nature places limits on all things, it also places boundaries to the existence of every human being. [7]

In matters of ultimate concern, Cicero's general optimism sustains him to the end. He looks forward to leaving the corruptions of this world and being reunited with those whom he has loved, including the son who predeceased him. While admitting that his hopes may be unfounded, this great humanist was satisfied that what he believes about what occurs after death has made this life a happy one. Unfortunately, his life was terminated by violence.

Let us turn to another important thinker about old age from that period: Pliny the Younger, who lived into the first century A.D. Pliny was a well-educated aristocrat and held important administrative positions. While he understood the grim realities of aging, he was drawn to the ideals expressed by Cicero. Because of early tragedies, Pliny had a multi-generational upbringing. He was always surrounded by people older than himself who helped nurture his development and had a positive influence upon his life and career. Pliny's older friends became a tangible means for him to reinforce his feelings about himself. [8]

---

7. *On Old Age*, Part IV.

8. Robert Kebric, "Aging In Pliny's Letters: A View from the Second Century A.D. 23," *The Gerontologist* 5, 539-47.

As Pliny matured, he made himself available for advice to those now coming after him. He also had definite views about how those able to retire should conduct their lives. Measure and tranquility were essential. When the elderly lived orderly lives, it gave Pliny a pleasure comparable to his contemplation of the fixed course of the planets. And to avoid obsolescence, he recommends that the old should continue to engage in projects that would be useful to the community as well as to themselves.

Seneca was another important thinker of Antiquity who studied the phenomenon of aging. He had many of the qualities of Cicero, being both philosopher and statesman. Like Pliny, Seneca lived into the first century of the Christian era. Seneca was from Spain and served under Nero, who ordered him to commit suicide. In his *Divine Comedy*, Dante places Seneca in limbo, treating him as a humanist saint, because of his non-Christian conformity to a simple life and belief in Divine Providence.[9]

Seneca left no treatise on Old Age, but made many references to it in his voluminous writings. Much of it repeats and expands upon what Cicero had written. And it is even more enthusiastic about this final stage of life. Seneca believed that we should embrace old age. It is, he says, full of pleasure if we know how to use it. In fact, old age is, of itself, a new pleasure, even though it eliminates the delights of the past. It is to be enjoyed, and not simply endured. None are never so old that it would be wrong for them to hope for another day. However, those who reach old age without leading an orderly and productive life are likely to suffer more than those who paid due attention to every step in their lives.

Like Cicero, Seneca insisted upon the use of the mind. Even as the body declines, the mind can retain its vigor. The last years of life are the best time for intellectual pursuits. As age increases, the mind flowers. It finds more meaning through thought because it has more leisure. Seneca even claimed that learning and study is better than travel; an assertion that today may be disputed.

9. Seneca, Epistle 12: " . . . That man is happiest and is secure in his own possession of himself who can await the morrow without apprehension." On Dante's view of Seneca's fate, see *The Inferno,* Canto IV (The Virtuous Pagans).

Seneca introduces a relatively new idea into the adventure of aging: concern for others. He notes that as we grow into maturity we benefit from the example and counsel of others, and he insists that we, in turn, must be willing to help others. We should give special attention to those who suffer from the infirmities of body and mind or are being consumed by inescapable loneliness. Seneca stated the point with emphasis: "You must live for another if you are to live for yourself."[10]

Medieval Europe and the Renaissance

Beginning with Plato, we have inherited from the ancient worlds of Greece and Rome many basic ideas about what it means to grow old. While these reflections seem to be of enduring benefit, some of them have been devalued by modern criticism. For example, doubts have been raised about the originality of Cicero's classic treatise, and we now know more of how others of that time felt that old age was a great burden. Moreover, the upper-class males who had the leisure to reflect upon the meaning of growing old, did not share the brutal fate of those of advanced years who lacked their resources or social position. Yet in spite of such qualifications, those ancient ideas of aging have had a lasting influence upon Western cultural history. We can detect some of that influence in the development of Christian civilization. [11]

The great poet of the late Middle Ages, Dante Alighieri, is best known for his classic *The Divine Comedy* which traces the passages of the soul through the symbolic realms of Hell, Purgatory, and Paradise. But Dante wrote widely on many other subjects including that of age. This topic is addressed in a late, unfinished work written early in the fourteenth century, called *Convivio* or

---

10. See, Lydia Motto, "Seneca On Old Age," *Estudios Latinos* 19 (2000) 128-39.

11. For criticism of Cicero, see Maria S. Hayes, "The Supposed Golden Age For The Aged in Ancient Rome: A Study of Literary Concepts of Old Age," *The Gerontologist* 11 (1963) 126-35.

The Banquet. This treatise has been called a hymn of love to philosophical wisdom.

Dante was what is called a Neoplatonist. He believed that our minds were capable of comprehending the whole of the created universe, which he thought of as a multiplicity that proceeded *downward* from the supreme unity that existed in the mind of God. As he applied that conceptual structure to the study of man, it allowed him to interpret the human condition in terms of various stages of nobility.

Since the time of Hesiod the successive periods of human life had been designated as specific ages, usually with a quasi-divine beginning and ending in a degradation of man. For Dante, there were four ages of man: *Adolescence, Youth, Old Age, and Decrepitude*. The first covered the time of life until approximately age twenty-five. During that time the soul concentrates upon the improvement of the body, while being outwardly obedient and modest. The second stage, *Youth*, lasted about twenty years. It was the most important stage, because it was the time of what we would call the growth into maturity. This period of human life –until about age forty-five—is one of a self-centeredness that is not neurotic. Rather, according to Dante, during this period the developing individual is trying to perfect his own inner powers, especially those of reason. His nobility lies in his quest for rational perfection, although he is also temperate, courteous, and loyal. Being at the center of the circle of life, *Youth* can look both backwards and forwards. The 'young' man must love his elders; because it is from them that he has received his being, his nourishment and instruction. It would be ignoble not to be grateful. He should also care for those who are his juniors, giving them a taste of the good things that he himself is now acquiring and, in later years, justifiably receive their assistance.[12]

Dante conceives of all the ages of life as arches of ascent and descent. There is no unqualified progression; within each stage there are advances and retreats. This is true also of *Old Age*, which for Dante begins at about forty-five years and lasts to around

12. *The Banquet*, Bk. IV. Ch. XXIII.

seventy. During this time some of the refinements of life, such as courtesy, begin to fade and gravity of demeanor begins to ascend. Obedience and Loyalty remain as virtues, but Dante expects that the elderly will comply spontaneously with such responsibilities. More importantly, moral values that were only dimly perceived at an earlier stage of life now come into clearer focus.

The elderly have a much fuller understanding of justice, seeing it now in its full complexity. It is not just a matter of reciprocal fairness between individuals. Like Aristotle, the old are aware that justice establishes the fair relations between the individual and the community as well as the rights and duties that individuals hold with respect to each other. The common good has a positive meaning. Those of advanced years understand more fully what is due to the whole as well as to one another. And with a wisdom informed by charity, Dante sees the elderly as affable, able to rejoice in the happiness of others. The contrast with Aristotle's dimmer view of the character of old men is striking. [13]

A noble old man is prudent in his judgments. The advantage of age is that at this point in life one has a good understanding of what is both past and present, and out of that knowledge can make wise predictions about the future. Dante insists that the old are wise, not just astute. And the perfection of prudence within them will lead others, as well as themselves, to that plenitude of good that is the object of living.

In the imaginative philosophy of Dante, there is a magnanimity at work in the soul of the noble old man; an inward benevolence that must expand beyond itself. Dante goes so far as to suggest that a good old man does not wait to be asked to give advice. This may make us wince, since we strongly believe in the rights to self-determination. But we should try to understand Dante's vision of a human nature that is ultimately oriented to God. He thought that Aristotle's understanding of human nature was too static and that the Greek philosopher was unable to grasp the depths of what it means to be a fully developed human being.

---

13. Ibid., Ch. XXVII.

For this was now a Christian age. In the transformations wrought by the reign of Revelation, a progression towards the higher virtues goes hand in hand with biological decline. The old are not just "senior citizens". They are, as the Spanish say, *Adultos Mejores*; human beings at a better stage of maturity, progressing towards the higher virtues in a manner that surpasses the earlier stages of life. There is now, or should be, an altruism, a perfection that "enlightens not only one's self but others." In a beautiful image Dante says that old age "should make a man open out, as it were, like a rose which can no longer keep closed, but must give forth the fragrance generated within it."[14]

Dante drew upon the medical knowledge of his time, so he observes that as one approaches the end of life, there is a decline in heat and an increase in moisture that is less easily evaporated. Now about ten years remain, more or less. This last stage is *Decrepitude*.

Like the Ancients, we are inclined to think of infirmity primarily in terms of physical decline. But Dante had a more spiritual and metaphysical idea in mind. The highest desire in all of nature is a return to its source and by this he does not mean a retreat to the womb but rather a final ascent to God. To express this ultimate idea Dante uses an image that would often be repeated in the literature: that of the sailor returning to port. As a good sailor nearing the harbor lowers his sails and carefully enters his destination, so should the noble soul in his final years drop off his worldly occupations and give his mind and heart to the contemplation of the divine. In such a spirit, he shall enter the last haven with great gentleness and peace.[15]

The poetic vision of a noble old age articulated by Dante was never realized in medieval civilization. Charlemagne lived to a meaningful old age, but a class of old people as such did not exist. For the peasants, thirty was considered to be a considerable age. Real old age was rare and when it did exist it was pitied or feared. There was much warfare and the weak and vulnerable were often ignored. There was a practical preference for the physical strength

14. Ch. XXVII .2.
15. Ibid. Ch. XXVIII.

of the young. Worse, a more pessimistic attitude towards the real infirmities of aging was beginning to develop.[16]

The Roman poet Horace, who flourished during the Augustan period, had written about the various stages of life, such as the playfulness of childhood, the irresponsibility of youth, and the ambitions of maturity. But for him old age was best described as being "full of inconveniences". As one interested in the erotic, Horace lamented the frigidity of old men who were foolish enough to fall in love. And in general, he thought that their character was not admirable. They quarreled and were miserly and their love of the past was matched only by their condemnations of the present. Subsequent elegies on old age placed special emphasis upon the loss of sexual potency, forgetting Cicero's advice that as the years go by, sensual decline can be replaced by different pleasures. And the realities of physical decay were increasing obvious. The drying up of the skin and the increasing colorlessness of the face were clear proofs of the ravages of age, as were the rheumy excesses of moisture in the eyes and nostrils. To the great physician Galen (circa 129-200), the signs of old age were analogous to the withering of a plant.

The assessments of the later years of life by religious authorities was also not encouraging. Pope Innocent III, (1198-1216) was one of the most powerful and influential personalities of the medieval period. He was famous for promoting crusades and disciplining the faithful. But he also wrote—before assuming the Papacy — a general treatise entitled *De Contemptu Mundi Sive de Miseria Humanae Conditionis* (1189). The work has been described as 'Swiftian' in its contempt for the physicality of human life.

Base from birth, the repulsiveness of man increases with age. *De Contemptu* includes dismal enumerations of the physical consequences of old age such as the rotting teeth, the shaking head and the stinking breath. The degeneracy was social as well as personal. The old talk too much and listen not enough. They are inclined to despise their contemporaries while praising their companions

---

16. Simone de Beauvoir, *The Coming of Age*, Patrick O'Brien, trans. (New York, G. P. Putnam, 1972), Ch. 3.

from long ago. Contemptuous of the present and clinging to what has passed, they become full of fear and anxiety.[17]

In the mind and heart of this great churchman, the world to come is given greater primacy than the reality of temporal existence. And his conception of life as a testing ground or pilgrimage was a reflection of the general Christian culture of his time. There was little chance for happiness on earth and even less for salvation. The sober theme of *momento mori* was replacing the stoicism of Roman paganism. The optimism of Cicero and Seneca, and even those of Dante about the positive possibilities of growing old was seemingly forgotten. Nonetheless, the more unfavorable attitude adopted by the church should not be exaggerated. Granted, the fear of hell compelled all believers to turn from evil, and the elderly could not be granted a moral exemption. But in medieval sermons the old were reminded that the advanced years could be useful to the spirit, even as they brought misery to the body. [18]

St. Augustine's promise of perpetual youth in Christ was especially comforting. While he insisted that at all stages of life one must seek repentance, faith implied hope, because the Paschal Mystery had restored the joy of our youth. Those who retained evil dispositions had to be warned of their ultimate peril, but those who led good lives were held in high esteem. According to Aquinas, honoring an aged man was a matter of justice, part of the respect owed to every human person who led a virtuous life. And youth and old age could co-exist within a single human soul that possessed qualities of quickness and gravity.

Questions of longevity were also addressed. The controversial Franciscan Roger Bacon (1220-1292) was known for the advances that he made in experimental science. As a theologian, he believed that the prevailing shortness of human life was not divinely

---

17. *Two Views of Man: Pope Innocent III, One, The Misery of Man Giannozzo Manetti, On the Dignity of Man,* Bernard Murchard, trans. (New York: Frederick Unger, 1966).

18. Shulamith Shahar, *Growing Old In The Middle Ages,* Yoel Lotan, trans. (New York: Routledge, 1997); Herbert Covey, "Old Age Portrayed by the Ages of Life Models from the Middle Ages to the 16th Century," *The Gerontologist* 5 (1989) 692-98.

ordained. Admitting the limits of natural life, and the corruptions we inherit from our parents, Bacon was nevertheless convinced that human beings could live much longer lives if they could only grasp the fundamentals of organic being and adopted for themselves a regime of healthful living. Although the wise men of the past did not understand these potentials, 'ere long' such capacities will be within the range of ordinary knowledge.[19]

While certain positive appraisal of the circumstances of the older members of the community gained some traction in the late Middle Ages, morbid images of old age persisted in the literature. *The Canterbury Tales* of Geoffrey Chaucer, published in the fourteenth century, provide some good examples. In *The Prologue to the Reeve's Tale*, old men are likened to fruit that grows worse with age: "We never ripen until we are rotten." The dreary situation is more vividly illumined with analogies drawn from the coals of a fire. The Reeve lists four 'coals' of old men: boasting, fibbing, anger, and greed. A more powerful metaphor is that of a cask running dry:

> The day I was born a long time ago,
> death opened up the spigot of my life and left it on.
> And ever since that day the old tap has just run
> And run
> Until now the barrel is practically empty.

In the period of Renaissance some edifying conceptions of old age emerged. In the imaginary work *Utopia (1516)* by Thomas More, the uncertainties surrounding old age are not relieved and of itself the condition is thought of as a disease. Yet More stressed the gravity and the reverence that was due to the elderly. In this imaginative work old men are honored with particular respect and the oldest man in every family was its governor. Great care is given to those who fall seriously ill, though if the pain becomes unbearable, voluntary euthanasia was an option.[20]

---

19. Friar Bacon, *His Discoveries of the Miracles of Art, Nature, and Magic* (London: Simon Miller, 1659).

20. Thomas More, *Utopia* Bk. II (1516).

In Elizabethan drama pessimism about the prospects of old age begins to color the general understanding of this final phase of life. *King Lear* is too old to learn, and his plight portrays the helplessness of an old leader whose need for guidance by others is palpable. As Sonnet 73 describes it, with advancing years there are "Bare ruined choirs/ where late the sweet birds sang." In Shakespeare's play *As You Like it,* the world is seen as a stage in which all the men and women are merely players. Life has seven stages, beginning with infancy, then schooling, moving on to lover and soldier "seeking the bubble reputation in the mouth of a cannon." Then comes a period of conventional success, "with eyes severe and beard of formal cut," soon to be followed by a sixth stage of gradual decline, "when the hose no longer fits the shank and a manly voice starts to turn to childish treble." Finally comes the last stage of all, ending this strange history, a "second childishness and mere oblivion/sans teeth, sans eyes, sans taste, sans everything."[21]

The poetry and drama of Shakespeare seems to cancel the positive possibilities of aging that had once flowed from Dante's imagination. The same pessimism is given more reflective expression in the Essays of Michel de Montaigne (1533-1592). In the famous Essay 57, Montaigne argued that it is unreasonable to expect to die of loss of powers brought on by extreme old age. Death by old age is rare, being as an exemption granted by nature "by special favor to a single person in the space of two or three centuries." The problem is not that the old do not keep working; it is that the young do not have enough employment opportunities to display their considerable talents. "As for me," said Montaigne, "I think that our souls are as developed at twenty as they are ever to be and give the promise of all that they can do . . . . Of all the beautiful actions possible, the most are performed before the age of thirty". After that period he would concede that, if time has been well spent, knowledge and experience can grow. But important qualities such as vivacity and quickness are diminished. These insights of Montaigne would come to fruition some three hundred years later

---

21. *As You Like It*, Act II, scene VII.

when we started the transition from a rural to an industrial society and the elderly begin to be excluded from manual activities.

A more balanced view can be found in the thought of the great English scientist and statesman, Sir Francis Bacon (1561-1626). In one of his essays, he returned to the ancient theme of the relation between youth and age. He enumerates the virtues and vices of each extreme. The young are fitter to invent than to judge, for execution than for counsel, and more capable with new projects than for settled business. Yet they are inclined to grasp for more than they can hold. Age has many faults, including that of being content with the "mediocrity of success", but it also has positive values, especially in the powers of understanding. Bacon suggests that the virtues of either age can correct the faults of both. [22]

The Coming of the Modern World

As we move more closely to the modern age, hopeful signs about growing old begin to appear. Some were dramatic. The great German humanist Johann Goethe (1749- 1832) was able to complete an extended span of life in the fields of science, government, and the arts. Novels and poetry flowed from his pen over long periods of time. As an octogenarian he was able to complete the second part of the drama *Faust*, the work by which he is best known. Goethe filled his long life through the unfolding of his inner powers by growth and rejuvenation. He gave his creative span of years a wholeness that denies the pessimism of Shakespeare and Montaigne.

In a last letter to a friend Goethe explained his personal philosophy. He believed that all men have a basic destiny, or character, that matures by absorbing, improving, and enhancing all that constitutes his life experience. Although threatened from time to time by serious illnesses, Goethe renewed his energy with great appetite for food and drink, as well as seemly endless love affairs. His mind was Germanic: comprehensive in its range and driven by

---

22. Sir Francis Bacon, "Of Youth and Age," in *The Essays of Francis Bacon* (Peter Pauper Press), 165.

a unifying desire. He sought to draw the whole world into himself so that he could, in return positively influence that world.

In his last years Goethe maintained in interest in life that extended far into the future. And that curiosity encompassed many of the problems of world commerce and transportation that are now the stuff of global politics. Goethe wrote of the importance of such a broad outlook in one of his late aphorisms:

> He whose vision cannot cover
> History's three thousand years
> Must in outer darkness hover
> Live within the day's frontiers.[23]

Important insights into old age arose again in Great Britain. In the middle of the Eighteenth century the distinguished English man of letters, Samuel Johnson, published a number of essays on the subject. Like Francis Bacon, Johnson gave special attention to the relationships between young and old.

The traditional idea was that those of early years would profit from the wisdom of the elderly, and that such relationships would be mutually beneficial. For Johnson, the prospects were less encouraging. For the ideas of two generations are so vastly different that they cannot be reconciled. The young look to the future; the old to the past. The young have hopes that the seniors cannot share. Consequently, the conversations between them generally end with one side or other feeling either contempt or pity.[24]

Vigorous youth quickly leave behind " . . . the phlegmatic sediment of weariness and deliberation and burst out in temerity and enterprise." They can be contemptuous of the elderly who try to imitate or compete with them. However, though the contrariness of Winter and Spring can never be fully united, mutual tenderness and respect can draw the extremes of age closer together. Johnson believed that with paternal affection the elderly could bear patiently with the foibles of youth. And the young can honor

---

23. See the introductory essay by Thomas Mann to *The Goethe Treasury, Selected Prose and Poetry* (Dover, 2006), xli.

24. *The Rambler*, #69, 1/13/1750.

the wisdom of older men, not by the pretense of friendship, but when the young clearly understand their seniors to be " . . . at a distance from them in the ranks of existence." [25]

Dr. Johnson also had some ideas about retirement. He put the issue bluntly: If you do not voluntarily leave the active life, at some point you shall be driven from it. . Best to leave the "full-peopled world" as soon as it was financially possible to do so. But the isolation of retreat could be dreadful. Unless one has funds, and some domestic support, the old man will find himself " . . . neglected or insulted in the midst of multitudes." [26]

And so how can one find a deeper happiness in old age? One way is by devotion, to individuals or causes, so long as it is given rather than received. And for this devout Anglican, piety was indispensable. Without religious hopes the final season of life will become flooded with despair. To drive home this point, Johnson draws on military metaphors. We should always be prepared for death, as we would, as a soldier, be constantly on alert for a siege. But to be unprepared for death in old age "is to sleep at an attack."[27]

Nineteenth century England experienced an increasing need for the institutional support of the aged. There were various causes, the principal one being the disappearance of large extended families that had once provided intergenerational support. As the young migrated to larger cities or to the vast domains of Empire, the old were often left to fend for themselves. They were becoming the wards of public largesse and private charities. The effects were depressing. Abandoned by the intimate domestic sphere, the elderly rapidly contracted their range of interests. Their deeper faculties were degraded by a lack of mental stimulation and, as they

---

25. *The Rambler*, #50, 9/8/50.

26. *The Rambler*, #69, 11/16/50. In writing of anger, rather than lust, as the chief vice of the elderly, Johnson remarks that the old man who is habitually peevish soon finds " . . . the world falls off from around him and he is left . . . .to devour his own heart in solitude and contempt.'" *The Rambler*, #11, 04/24/1750.

27. *The Rambler*, #50, 12/15/50.

became increasing lethargic, they desired no more than warmth and food.[28]

In the Victorian age, some of the positive features of old age gained attention, in part because of the example of elderly public figures such as the Queen and Gladstone. The major poets also had their opinions. Browning's urging, "Come grow old with me/the best is yet to be," gained a wide audience, and Tennyson inspired many of advancing years to keep trying for some accomplishment so that they should not " . . . rust unburnished, not to shine in use." The poem, "Ulysses," expresses the basic philosophy of the poet:

> . . . [Y]ou and I are old;
> Old age has yet his honor and his toil;
> Death closes all: but something ere the end,
> Some work of noble note, may yet be done,
> Not unbecoming men that strove with Gods. [29]

Unfortunately, the judgment of the poets on the subject of old age was not uniformly optimistic. For Matthew Arnold, "*Growing Old* meant loss of form, beauty and strength—and worse. There were no 'golden days' and we lose all feeling that we were ever young. In the last stage it is to be "frozen up within, and quite/the phantom of ourselves . . . ."[30]

The most radical pessimism was produced by the novelist Anthony Trollope. In 1882 he published a novel entitled *The Fixed Period*. It imaginatively describes an island that was formerly a British colony that, after gaining independence, attempted to abolish the misery of old age and state expenditures for the elderly. The government adopted a policy of forced retirement at age 67, followed by a year of reflection that ended with a humane form of euthanasia. In the novel, the plan is thwarted by Imperial intervention, but, as we shall see, the idea provoked a wider controversy.

---

28. Karen Chase, *The Victorians and Old Age* (Oxford: Oxford University Press, 2009).

29. Alfred Lord Tennyson, Ulysses (1842).

30. Matthew Arnold (1822-1888) was the son of the famous educator, Thomas Arnold. *Growing Old* was published in 1867, some twenty years before Matthew Arnold's death.

Other writers dealt with the conflict between the middle-class promise of a comfortable old age and the challenge of heroic efforts called for by Tennyson. In her novels, Margaret Oliphant explored the differences between a 'static aesthetic' and a vital, generative condition. The problem with old age, even when not accompanied by financial distress, was that it left the aging individual living in a phase of the life cycle that was different in kind, and not just in degree, from all the others. As maturity turns into very old age, the isolation intensifies even when one has the company of others similarly situated.

The mutual reliance of the very old upon each other occurs within a closed circle of conversation. Bitterness and gossip become a collective form of self-enclosure. The poison of selfishness is refined. So what are the alternatives? Isolation makes matters worse; the only constructive options are intergenerational. Encounters with the young are risky, but social ties across generations can be of great benefit to all concerned. The trajectory of age is more satisfying when age does not diminish youth, nor youth avoid, or try to abolish age. The hope was for humanistic amplitude in which men and women of all ages are integrated in important public as well as private events.[31]

Some blamed the excesses of capitalism on the sorrows of old age. On the political plane, an Old Age Pensions Act sought to bring public policy into line with the lived experience of the elderly. Artists looked more deeply into the corrosive effects of unbridled materialism on the prospects for constructive labor and leisure among the aging population. To that end, William Morris looked retrospectively to what he considered was a more satisfactory historical period; that of the Middle Ages.

In that earlier age crafts prevailed, and men made objects that were beautiful as well as useful. And they took pleasure in

---

31. *The Victorians and Old Age*, Ch. 3. In one of his reflections on aging Johnson paid particular attention to the circumstances of elderly women. Their neglect shows that to society at large that their beauty has faded and their power and value have been lost. Consequently, they are left with a " . . . .tedious and comfortless uniformity of time, without any motion of the heart or exercise of the reason. *The Rambler*, #69, 11/13/1750.

their work. Industrialization and mechanization swept those values aside and increased the prospects of unemployment especially among those lacking the physical strength of the young. Morris believed that if the debilitating effects of modern life were removed, premature aging would cease. A revival of simpler trades as well as a mainly pastoral existence would allow men to remain able and vigorous late into life and the young and old would become virtually indistinguishable.[32]

Back on the continent, a French writer, Emile Souvestre, published *The Pleasures of Old Age* (1868). He lamented the fact that many of his countrymen were fearful of old age He sought to persuade them that the advanced years were not as dreadful as they imagined. Old age, he argued, does not put down life; it perfects it.[33]

True, we are now removed from the active life of society. But we have special seats as spectators from where we can follow the drama with tranquil mind and begin to understand the real value of everything. With sufficient perception and good will we shall find that all around us can gladden and engage our lives. Those so inclined can attend to the broader interests of the human family, but there are also great pleasures to be experienced close to home. Watching others pass by one's windows awakens memories and inspires new sympathies. Music provides the charms of indefinite expression. Even the receipt of a letter provides new pleasures. One need not just skim the message; in this period of life we can see the missive as imparting something of a human soul that has traveled many miles to reach its reader. [34]

---

32. Morris's views of the future were of a socialist society. See his *News From Nowhere* (1890). His utopian ideas bear some comparison with the American futurist Edward Bellamy and his work *Looking Backward* (1887).

33. " . . . Old age has a charm in my eyes because it has brought me the independence which is the reward of labor, together with the experience which teaches me how to enjoy it, the moderation which economizes our pleasures, and the leisure which enables us to appreciate them. . . . " *The Pleasures of Old Age*, at 32.

34. Chapter VI.

Souvestre also gains great enjoyment from rereading the classics. He now finds new insights and details that he had previously overlooked. The deepening comprehension seems to make very sun rise higher in the sky. And his library is now dearer to him. Once it was just a collection of so many volumes. Now they are filled with life:

> The spirit enshrined within these pages has come forth to meet my own. I have found in them inquirers who have committed to me their thoughts; friends who have taken possession of me, and introduced me into the inner circle of their lives. Incomparable society ever ready to receive me; inexhaustible friendship that will never fail me, which waits only for my initiative to afford me sympathy and delight.[35]

From Colonial to Industrial America

Let us now turn to the New World. We begin with the Puritans of colonial New England. Puritanism was a branch of Calvinism, a form of Protestantism which placed great stress upon the wisdom of the Old Testament, including its understanding of old age. So it was not unusual that this last stage of life was given considerable respect and even veneration among our first settlers. Old age was a sign of God's favor. According to the theologian Cotton Mather, the elderly had "a peculiar acquaintance with the Lord Jesus Christ, an acquaintance that verged on likeness". The honoring of old age in the Scripture was endlessly repeated in these Seventeenth century sermons, even thought old persons made up only about two percent of the population. While positive precepts applicable to the elderly in colonial New England were derived from the Hebrew bible, Scripture also formed a basis to criticize the failures and vices of those at an advanced stage of life. An early critique found the elderly too tenacious for the things of this world, full of suspicion, and very apt to fear the worst. The preachers reminded

---

35. *The Pleasures of Old Age*, 313.

them that they must attend more closely to the things of God and cultivate within themselves habits of temperance, sobriety, and charity.[36]

In the poetry of that period, the limitations of aging were even more imaginatively described. Anne Bradstreet, a great New England poet, expressed her reflections upon Old Age in a way similar to the pessimistic appraisal of Shakespeare. She divided the drama of human life into four acts, and the last to come upon the stage was Old Age, "leaning upon his staff." He carried a harvest of great abundance, but in one hand he held a glass: "ev'n almost run/ thus writ about: this out and I am done." And, instead of the "sans everything" of Shakespeare, Bradstreet was more specific:

> My grinders now are few, my sight doth fail
> My skin is wrinkled and my cheeks are pale
> My hands and arms, once strong, have lost their might
> I cannot labor, nor can I fight[37]

Some of the difficulties that accompanied old age were relieved by the closeness of family life. All the members of society, old as well as young, could be maintained within one household or within residential proximity. This made for closer contacts between generations. Many children had an intimate experience of the wisdom and doings of the old. And the preachers assured the elderly that even if their families grew weary of them, God would not abandon them.

In this pre-modern society the elderly had a greater place in the social structure than is the case in our time. They held important political and religious offices. They also held valuable economic resources, especially land, and their presumed closeness to God gave them an enviable personal status. They had authority and confidence in both their words and their carriage. But if they

---

36. David Hackett Fischer, *Growing Old In America* (1975); John Demos, "Old Age in Early New England," 84, *The American Journal of Sociology Supplement* 1 (1978) 5248-5287.

37. Anne Bradstreet was born in England in 1612 and came to America with her father aboard John Winthrop's ship *The Arbella*. "Old Age" is part of a longer poem on the ages of man. She died in September of 1672.

were respected, it was more a matter of awe than affection. Moreover, resentment and ridicule was gradually being directed towards them. Their vices were detestable because they were visible. Old age brought an exposure that had previously been protected by a veneer of custom and religious practices. Nearness did not assure closeness and harmony, even though the preachers warned that to deride aged persons was a great sin.

Hostility toward the elderly increased after the Revolution. In the period between the last quarter of the eighteenth and first quarter of the nineteenth centuries, there was a change of attitude towards them. A distancing indifference was developing in the minds of the younger members of society. Ideals of rank and seating by age in church were abandoned. Family responsibility for the aged declined and old age homes made available for those too old to care for themselves. As land became more available westward, the young no longer had to wait in expectation to inherit the ancestral farm.[38]

The moral authority of the elders was being swept away by the democratic principles of equality and terms of disrespect such as 'geezer' or 'old goat' became part of the common vocabulary. In the famous *Walden* Thoreau asserted that whenever a senior tells you that you cannot do something, if you try, you find that you can. There was little to be learned from the elderly and his motto for this maturing society was: "Old deeds for old people and new deeds for new". Nevertheless, by the middle of the nineteenth century, there was developing in New England a renaissance of arts and letters that would manifest a residual respect for old age.[39]

Ralph Waldo Emerson, philosopher, essayist, and poet wrote in favor of aging. Emerson had read Cicero's classic and gave the ideas of the great Roman a new and forceful restatement. Emerson was one of the Transcendentalist, those who believed that the most important knowledge existed beyond the senses and were convinced of the spiritual unity of all that exists. These principles directed Emerson's understanding of old age. Those who despised the elderly because of their visible shortcomings were not getting

---

38. Fischer, op. cit.
39. *Walden* (1854), Ch. 1.

at the deeper truth, because they did not understand, as Emerson did, that true value is inward. The essence of age is intellect and its powers compensate for many physical problems. Conceding that in this country the estimate of age has become low and skeptical, Emerson asserted that such opinions flow from urban streets and markets and "the haunts of pleasure and gain." Age, like woman, needs fit surroundings. It is becoming in the country, not in "the rush and uproar of Broadway". Age has its advantages. Life and art are cumulative and those who have accomplished something important earlier in life are still entitled to be heard. [40]

The universal prayer for a long life, which both nature and history confirm, admonishes the ridicule of age. Emerson rejects the idea promoted by Montaigne that the soul matures early in life. That was too limited a conception of the development of human nature. Those who are old in a substantial sense are not the cartoonish and peevish dotards- the falsely old—but rather noble men "who fear no city and by whom cities stand".

The great deeds of old men were part of American history especially in the lives of eminent persons such as Benjamin Franklin and John Adams. Emerson had visited Adams in 1825 and found him, even in extreme old age, still worthy of his fame. In science, there was the example of Newton, who made important discoveries for many of his eighty-five years. Throughout history, in every field of human endeavor, the elderly had proven the truth of Cicero's dictum, that without the old there is no civilization.

The old are often said to be fearful, but Emerson preferred to observe how age brings release from fears. Even one who reaches sixty is thankful for the calamities he has avoided. And then there is the release from disordered passions that has been noted since ancient times. In our younger years we live among a rabble of conflicting desires, but when the interiors of mind and heart are opened, our actions are supplied with higher motives. Even in our professional or business lives we experience emancipation. As we reach the furthest boundaries of maturity, our reputations become

---

40. Ralph Waldo Emerson, "Old Age." *The Works of Ralph Waldo Emerson*, vol. 2 (Society and Solitude) Fireside Edition (Boston/New York, 1909).

established; as we move further on we tend to disregard the opinions of others. With the coming of advanced years a great weight of degrading anxieties has been lifted.

In our earlier years we had to struggle to find adequate expression for our thoughts and feelings. But age compensates. As we grow older we are empowered "to say what we mean and mean what we say". The ferment of earlier years has submitted to a serenity of thought and action. Moreover, over time, our undeveloped ideas mature. When we are young, we start many projects and bring few to completion; a delight of age is that we are empowered to coordinate our thoughts and to finish that which we have begun. If our lives have been well spent, age is a loss of what can be well spared. We gain a real happiness when our mind is purified and wise and if we remember that whoever loves is in no way old. We are moving towards a life just ready to be born. In his famous poem *Terminus* Emerson returns to those nautical images through which old age has been so often described. He reminds us that even as we take in the sail, we can

> Right onward drive unharmed
> The port well worth the cruise is near
> And every wave is charmed.[41]

Other encouraging poetry came from this creative period. Longfellow wrote a poem about old age for his college reunion that bears some resemblance to Tennyson's *Ulysses*. In *Morituri Salutamus* the poet was unsparing in his recognition of the facts: This ultimate stage of life is "The dusk of evening/ not the blaze of noon." And when it comes, there is a loss of both strength and desire. Yet, unlike Matthew Arnold, this New England poet does not despair, but rather speaks words of encouragement:

> What then: Shall we sit idly down and say
> The night hath come, it is no longer day?
> The night hath not yet come; we are not quite

---

41. First published in 1866, there has always been some controversy over when it was written. See Carl F. Strauch, "The Date of Emerson's Terminus," *PMLA* 64.4 (June, 1950) 360-70.

Cut off from labor by the failing light;
Something remains for us to do or dare
Even the oldest tree some fruit may bear.
***
For age is opportunity no less
Than youth itself, though in another dress,
And as the evening twilight fades away
The sky is filled with stars, invisible by day.[42]

Oliver Wendell Holmes (1819-1894) was another important New England thinker who had valuable insights into the significance of old age. Holmes was a physician, writer, and father of the famous Supreme Court Justice, Oliver Wendell Holmes, Jr. The elder Holmes had pursued his interest in medicine by studying in Paris earlier in the century. Upon his return to his home near Boston, he became a lecturer, practitioner, and man of letters. He lived to the ripe old age of eighty nine.

One of his earlier publications was entitled *The Autocrat at the Breakfast Table* (1858), which was an immediate success as it mixed kindness and humor with depth of insight. It was in this work that Holmes made his most extensive comments on the subject of aging. He had also read Cicero's famous *De Senectute* and was impressed of its account of the great deeds done by men who had lived a long life. Holmes approached the subject of old age from a medical perspective, which, at that time, looked upon the human body as a furnace-burning carbon container. At about age forty-five those fires begin to slacken, so it is important to restore fuel by both eating and exercise. Holmes recommended horseback riding, walking, and especially rowing—an interesting emphasis since the use of rowing machines is now considered one of the best ways to maintain physical health. And even as the inevitable decline persists, Holmes recommends that the elderly remain gentlemen.[43]

---

42. The poem was delivered in 1875, the date of Longfellow's fiftieth reunion. The title means "We who are about to die salute you"—the Roman Gladiator's greeting to the Emperor. Longfellow died in 1882.

43. *The Autocrat of the Breakfast Table*. Ch. VII (1882).

Reflections On Old Age

Within a broader anthropology, Holmes had his own conception of the stages of life. He thought that there here were a good number of distinct periods, but the primary ones were infancy, childhood, youth, maturity, and old age. Within each classification there were three sub-divisions: immaturity, complete development, and decline. As for old age, Holmes thought it comes upon us virtually unnoticed. We become aware of the transition when we seek to strive and begin to remember. Youth gradually leaves and just as gradually we leave behind the feelings of immortality.

Holmes's skill as a writer is brought out in his description of an old man:

> . . . as a person with a smooth shining crown and a fringe of scattered white hairs, seen in the street on a sun-shining day, bearing a cane, moving cautiously and slowly; telling old stories, smiling at present follies, living in a narrow world of dry habits; one who remains waking when others have dropped off to sleep, and keeps a little night-lamp, burning year after year if the lamp is not upset.[44]

The 'dry habits' were a matter of concern. Holmes recognized the value of routines, since they helped a man get more out of less. But too many habitual practices show that a man has shrunk into himself and excludes all outside influences. This to Holmes was a moral deficiency. Like other New Englanders, Holmes believed deeply in individual freedom. The highest calling of our being is one of "perpetual self-determination" in a way that never fails to take account of and respond to all our existing circumstances. Habits infringe upon that liberty. The comment reminds one of Cardinal Newman's famous dicta that to be alive is to change and to change often is to become perfect.

Positive images of the value of old age continued into the period following the Civil War. Grandparents still made a substantial contribution to the raising of their grandchildren and longevity was considered to be a source of wisdom and happiness. But after 1870, the number of older persons rose considerably and their

44. Ibid.

contributions to the well being of society became more questionable. In the economy, increased industrialization with its emphasis upon speed and productivity diminished the value of more time-consuming occupations and crafts that were a primary source of income for senior citizens. Montaigne's assessment found its outlet. The young were increasingly seen as being the part of the population that had the most to give to progress through vitality and creative endeavors. The older a man was, the less he was expected to offer to general prosperity. In the emerging rationalization of business practices, the old were not esteemed for their wisdom and experience. They were devalued as being inefficient human machines.[45]

In 1905, the eminent Canadian born physician, William Osler, (1849-1919) gave a talk at the Medical School of Johns Hopkins University in which he made a humorous reference to Trollope's book *The Fixed Period,* in which, as we have seen, the British author had created an imaginary utopia that included a policy of forced retirement at age 67, followed by a year of reflection that would end with a humane form of euthanasia. Osler also gave as his opinion that the most important work is done between the ages of 25 and 40. After that "it is all downhill". Even worse, by sixty, a man was useless. Osler was accused in the press of promoting euthanasia, which he denied, but his remarks were a vivid expression of the deep changes that were taking place concerning the dignity of the older members of society.[46]

One important aspect of these changes was the attention being given to childhood, as a distinct phase of life. The strength and speed of the young was celebrated in the rise of organized athletics as well as in progress of industrialization. Within the family, the authority of grandparents, as well as that of parents, was diminished since, beginning with infancy, there was now greater dependence upon quasi-scientific external guidance. As the public

---

45. Peter N. Stearns, "The Obsolescence of Old Age In America 1865-1914," *Journal of Social History,* 8.1 (1974) 48-62.

46. William Osler "The Fixed Period," *Archives of International Medicine* 161.2; Sherwin B. Nuland, *The Art of Aging,* Ch.10 (2001).

educational system grew in importance, its purpose seemed to be more to delay, than to facilitate, the passage to adulthood. We were beginning to develop that cult of the young that was denounced by Chinese civilization.

As a result of these changes individuals, both young and old, began sharing values within their own age groups rather than across generations. The different age groups had less and less to say to each other. The consumer culture not only promoted the cult of the young, it also stressed the importance of a youthful appearance to the self-esteem of adults. There was a pervasive gerontophopia, an anxiety about aging that had not previously been part of the American experience. [47]

Ironically, during this changing cultural period that diminished the authority of age, life expectancy was increasing. By the beginning of the twentieth century men could expect to live to about 50; women a bit longer. But what *place* would they have in the new century and beyond? As youthful force and adaptability become guiding principles, were the more numerous elderly to be considered as encumbrances to be left behind? Beyond retirement, what contribution could these seniors reasonably make to the growth of both their families and the societies of which they remain a part? As Cicero asked, we may consider: what great actions remain to be done that do not depend upon physical strength or speed. And how could science and medicine not only improve the health of the aging population but also make possible the extension of life? As the new century developed, questions of longevity would become of greater importance to a society struggling to afford equal dignity to all its members.

---

47. Victoria Secunda, *By Youth Possessed: The Denial of Age in America* (New York: Bobbs-Merrill, 1894).

2

Longevity and the Science of Aging

The Twentieth Century: Increasing Life Expectancy

AS LATE AS THE sixteenth century average life expectancy in Western Europe was only between eighteen and twenty years. By the nineteenth century the length of life had increased to an average of thirty-eight years, and by the beginning of the twentieth century the average throughout the Western World was about fifty. There was public acknowledgment of the advance. Here in the United States *A Report on National Vitality* issued in 1909 noted the increase and attributed it to improved sanitation, vaccination, and other measures of public health. The report also observed that changes in education and the time necessary for career preparation had helped to create the need for a longer life. Optimistically, it predicted that the addition in the number of older men and women would not result in more invalids. Rather, it was hoped that the extension of life would give us a population that included many vigorous old men fully able to apply their intelligence and experience to the most complicated and most delicate social issues.

The *Report* also predicted that increased longevity would pay economic dividends. One cannot but wonder if this expectation was meant to counter the increased pressures upon older citizens to retire from active employment in order that the young could advance. Following the lead of President Theodore Roosevelt, the author of the *Vitality Report* claimed that the extension of human life would lead to a greater resourcefulness and inventiveness throughout the whole of American society. A program of promoting those ends was recommended, because such developments were the mark of a progressive nation. The *Report* also sought to establish a standard for 'normal' life expectancy by treating genuine old age as an anomaly that begins at about eighty-three years.

The dawn of the twentieth century also saw the beginnings of serious speculative reflections on the nature and purpose of old age. Nathaniel Shaler, a geological scientist and follower of the theories of evolution, published an important work titled *The Individual: A Study of Life and Death* (1901). Shaler defended the value of the individual throughout all aspects of organic existence. He made an important distinction between the life span of human beings and that of lower animals. In the sub-human world, the time between reproduction and death was brief, but for human beings, there was an expectation of meaningful existence after the time of sexual procreation. For the lower animals, longevity is burdensome to themselves and others of their species. For Shaler, what is important about human beings is that man is a speaking animal. As his time on earth is extended, relations between elder persons and those younger than themselves ought to expand, because those of advanced years possess a fund of wisdom and experience that gives them a distinctive place in the overall social network. Thus it is that the prolongation of life is of humanistic value.[1]

Although he was by training a scientist, Shaler had a distinct sense of the historical development of human societies. Each begins in a barbaric stage; a time marked by extensive conflict both within the group itself and with its neighbors. In these circumstances the elderly are of little or no account, because they are not fighters. A community will begin to place a distinct value upon its elderly only when it becomes more settled. Only then does the transmission of values and traditions become important to the common good. The elderly remember. More positively, they are 'readopted' into the broader society in order that they may bring to it the values that inhere in the gift of years. Unlike those who

---

1. Nathanial Southgate Shaler. *The Individual, A Study of Life and Death* (New York: D. A. Appleton, 1902).

are fully immersed in the active life, those living longer lives have the advantage of seeing the human adventure in the broadest possible terms. They bring to the general community an experiential feeling for the relative scale of values and an understanding of the significance of time that those of lesser age are too busy to grasp.

While those who are old are no longer able to bear arms, they comprehend the follies and adverse consequences of war, since they have probably already lived through times of conflict. And although they may be less efficient or agile than those who are younger, there are still productive tasks that they can perform. According to Shaler, the important thing is to draw the elderly into closer association with the rest of society. Not only do they contribute to the vitality of the total organism; when they receive proper respect, they can bridge the gaps between successive generations. The elderly give to life in association a sense of wholeness that is lost whenever they are cast aside and excluded from what is considered to be important.

G. Stanley Hall was another thinker of the early twentieth century who believed that not enough intelligence has been devoted to an understanding of old age. Hall was a prominent psychologist and the president of an important university. Ironically, he had made his reputation in an earlier study on the subject of adolescence. But in 1922 he published a book titled *Senescence, or A study of the last half of life*. In it he brought together some of the most important and diverse observations on old age that had been made since the last years of the previous century.

Drawing on a wide range of previously published books and articles, Hall incorporated into his own work the thoughts of a variety of people who had already expressed ideas about the problems of growing old. There were, for example, comments by a retired teacher who believed that even in poverty and illness the old could be happy so long as they try to make "their corner of the world brighter." Hall also quoted one who had written that literary men live longer than mathematicians do "because imagination beats calculation." The same article-included admonitions to work in gardens and take long walks if one wished to live a long life. Another warned of the dangers of retiring into oneself.[2]

An article from *Harpers* magazine by the famous novelist W.D. Howells titled *Eighty Years and After* is cited by Hall for its insights into the virtues and failings of old age. Howells argued that those who have grown old should interest themselves more than they have in public questions. He also thought that women have a special talent for drawing the young and old together. A well-known scientist, H. D. Sedgwick, is quoted for the contrasts he draws between the lives of the young and the old. Sedgwick was convinced that the differences between old and young are particularly strong when it comes to an appreciation of beauty. He uses an interesting example: If a young man approaches a mountain, he fixes his eyes on the summit and begins to figure out how he will get there; an older man in the same situation will take delight in all the natural wonders of the total environment. The old are also more religious and less subject to emotional crises than the young. The elderly see "wonder in the iris", and they see God in the commonplace. And they also " . . . find beauty in cloud, flower and tree; while youth is too busy with its own emotions and their tyranny." As for the decline in activity, Sedgwick pointed out that it is the spectator in the theater who gets the most out of the drama.[3]

Another writer to whom Hall favorably refers had declared that in spite of his advanced years he refused to grow old. He criticizes his fellows who are constantly judging others. This makes them unpopular. He advises them to be positive and thereby increase the respect of those of lesser age. A correspondent with the *Atlantic Monthly* declared that, at 73, the seasons have never been so enjoyable. Nor did he fear death, because he believed that, when

---

2. G. Stanley Hall. *Senescence: The Last Half of Life* (London: D. Appleton, 1922). Ch. III. Hall's significance is discussed in Jill Lepore, "Twilight, Growing Old and Even Older," *The New Yorker*, March 14, 2011, 30-35.

3. "It is really the spectator in the theater who gets the most out of it. Youth is exclusive in its foolish divisions. The old do not dwell on differences but on common qualities. The old man finds no solace in isolation but in community . . . ." *Senescence*, 24.

it came, it would remove the final barrier between him and the fullness of life.

Hall thought that there were five stages to life: childhood, adolescence, middle age, senescence, and senectitude. In his conception, the middle years, or the prime of life, last until the early forties. At that time, senescence, or growing old, begins. This continues into the seventies, when senectitude, or old age as such, arrives. Like Oliver Wendell Holmes before him, G. Stanley Hall stressed the value of physical exercise as well as intellectual development as age increases. Personal hygiene was also important. But Hall warned that, as we give more attention to our physical being, we must be careful not to become hypochondriacs. And like Holmes, Hall emphasizes the importance of self-reliance. If we always strive to "do, be, and say" what is the best of us, we shall find not only respect but also companionship.[4]

As a psychologist, Hall realized that, as we grow older, our general attitude towards the experience of living undergoes some change. We should look out, not in, in order to resist self-centeredness. As we are beginning both to live longer and to retire earlier, the number of years we must take into account is extended. According to Hall, it is important that we do not understand senescence as a second childhood. In spite of Shakespeare's opinion, Hall does not think that growing old brings us back to the beginning of life. There is nothing rejuvenating about being elderly. Hall was a realist. He wanted us to understand that old age takes us by surprise, and that it is a stage of life that we neither grow out of nor are able to look back upon.

It is up to us to make something out of this terminal development. To effectively make his point, Hall uses some imaginative metaphors. He refused to think of old age in nautical terms, as Emerson had done. Senescence is not a harbor where we cast anchor and rest. Rather, as we age, we should think of ourselves as making landfall on a new continent. There we should be up and about, exploring our new surroundings, getting the lay of the land, and then embarking upon new adventures. Only by positively moving

4. Ibid., Ch. VIII.

forward can we acquire a complete understanding of the nature and purposes of our life on earth.

What is of particular interest about Hall's psychological approach to old age is that he views it in the context of the whole of human life. By taking such a broad view, he sees problems in human society that begin much earlier than the final stages of existence but continue into it. His central insight was that, in the emerging modern world, humanity *en masse* suffers from a pervasive immaturity. There is an arrested development at every stage of life. We are more conscious of this unadultness today, as commercial advertisements and the popular culture try to persuade us that an endless adolescence is the most we can hope for. As the saying goes, we can't avoid growing older, but we never have to grow up.[5]

Can senior citizens overcome this imperfection? Can old age be a time of ripening, of a maturity that the rest of human society has failed to attain? To use Dante's metaphor, can we ascend even as we decline; become complete and fully developed adults even as our bodies deteriorate? These are the major issues that Hall raises, and we would be wise to think carefully about his recommendations.

Part of his advice is paradoxical and even unsettling. He seems to suggest that as we become less important to the world we should not simply fall back upon our families for our satisfaction and security. But do we have any other alternatives? For Hall, the ultimate solution is personal. It concerns how all of us, by ourselves, experience our changing circumstances and what we are willing to do about it.

Hall assures us that, if we attend to simple pleasures, old age can be the most enjoyable time of our lives. But at the same time, we must cultivate an inner strength. If we have lost faith in the future, it is usually because we have lost faith in ourselves. Hall, like Holmes, wants us to be self-reliant. But he does not recommend isolation

---

5. "Both we and our civilization now so checked, disoriented, and misled by immaturities are in such crying need of a higher leadership that is not forthcoming! We suffer from . . . unripeness. The human stock is not maturing as it should." *Senescence*, 381.

from the community of others. Our neighbors can be a source of much happiness, if we take the time to reach out to them. Friendship is crucial. We should rejuvenate those friends of long tenure, create new ones, and, where necessary, heal old animosities.

Hall willingly acknowledges the various ways that women master the difficulties of old age. In comparison with men, a woman has a stronger hold on her youth, cares more for her appearance, and usually does not *feel* as old as men do. Women also deal better with loneliness. They are more sociable with each other, while a man is inclined to view another masculine presence as an intrusion upon his privacy.

Hall is probably the only serious thinker about old age who considers the relevance of marriage to the enjoyment of this final stage of life. Of course, time creates widows and widowers, and these tragedies can cause inconsolable sadness. Yet many married couples move together into a longer life, and the quality of their interpersonal relationship has a great deal to do with whether they must just endure, or can find pleasurable, these advanced years.[6]

This inevitably raises the question of sexuality. In spite of the claims of Viagra, senescence is the Indian summer of eroticism. Time takes a toll on such intimacies in even the happiest of unions. But for Hall, the decline of physical ardor is an opportunity for a married couple to move into a more mature love. The wise husband gains a new respect for the 'eternal feminine' that is represented in his wife. And friendship between spouses can improve, even as sexual activity declines.

At this point, a comparison with Cicero's treatise is instructive. Recall how this classical thinker believed that a loss of sensual pleasure was a gain for cerebral power. Through the centuries, many other men reflecting upon old age have reached similar conclusions. They promoted the idea that, once a man was freed

---

6. In spite of the difficulties, marriage is a hopeful state for those living into old age. Erotic attraction between a couple fades, but friendship between them can increase. As for the male, he has "... a new appreciation of the eternally feminine, its intuitive qualities, and its more general and moral interests ...." It is a great tragedy for a married couple not to grow old together. Ibid., 394-95.

from sensual passion, he can advance to more refined and solitary mental pleasures. But in the modern world, the heterosexual dimension of human experience has, for good and ill, gained greater currency. For Hall, addressing the nature of marriage, the decline of sexual intimacy creates an opportunity for a married couple to move into a more sublimated phase of reciprocal love. As the love between a husband and wife becomes more a matter of the soul than of the body, the partners can experience a more truly devoted union that, for both, enriches the time of old age.

Of course, those who remain wedded in their later years, or become married late in life, assume a double burden. For they must care for another as well as for themselves. Nonetheless, a married couple that, in spite of advancing years, pays attention to their life in common will gain a deeper understanding of the meaning of love. On such a firm foundation their separate lives will also flourish. Both, in their own way, will be able to improve upon the type of personality they possessed at an earlier stage of life. They will find themselves empowered to draw past, present, and future into a new and higher unity. Both become more magnanimous and reflective. Both become more complete moral beings, for it is only in marriage that the character can be fully developed. From a better understanding of what it means to grow old together, we may gain new insights into that most basic of humanistic problems: the nature of mature existence.[7]

The Report on National Vitality that was published early in the twentieth century envisioned that life extension would pay economic dividends, as elder citizens became more capable of making direct contributions to the industrial development of the country. However, there were also those who saw the prolongation of life as creating opportunities for older members of society to assume deeper and broader responsibilities to human life as a whole.

---

7. According to Hall, in old age we discover a 'new self' "... that both adds and subtracts much from the old personality of our prime . . . find compensation for what old age leaves behind in what it brings that is new . . . . So, when audition becomes less sensitive, we turn to the voices of inner oracles. If current events impress and absorb us less, we can knit up the past, present, and future into a higher unity." *Senescemce*, 403.

One whose thinking was moving in this more expansive direction was the Russian biologist Elie Metchnikoff.

Metchnikoff (1845-1916) was a member of the Pasteur Institute in Paris. He had won fame by being a co-recipient of the Nobel Prize for Chemistry in 1908 for his work on non-cellular immunities. Increasingly, he gave his attention to the problems of aging and the prospects for a meaningful life in the advanced years. Metchnikoff's humanistic work was in continuity with the organic optimism of Roger Bacon and a repudiation of Montaigne's view that old age was an exceptional circumstance. Metchnikoff's work on digestive and cardiovascular problems led him to conclude that, once diseases were suppressed and life hygienically controlled, death would come normally in extreme old age—a time when all the terror associated with the terminal event had been dissolved. During the extended life period, healthier conditions would assure that old men would no longer be subject to loss of memory or intellectual weakness. But they would not just be economically useful. The elderly would be empowered to apply their wisdom and great experience to the most complicated and delicate problems that might arise in any phase of modern social life.[8]

The outbreak of the First World War chilled the optimism of this creative scientist, because he realized that the extensive armed conflict would place scientific advancements in jeopardy. But the failure of statesmen to prevent the outbreak of hostilities in 1914 also deeply disturbed those of a more artistic sensibility. The dramatist George Bernard Shaw saw the war as a calamity that called out for greater efforts to promote longevity. That was because the failure to prevent or limit the conflagration revealed the immaturity of those who govern nations. Like Hall, Shaw had a sense of arrested development. Even the oldest men were not living long enough to resolve the general difficulties of keeping order, particularly those of international relations. Shaw's insights echoed Cicero's dictum that without those who are old there can be no civilization.

8. Elie Metchnikoff. "The Nature of Man." *Studies in Optimistic Philosophy* (1905).

Shaw expressed his ideas in a five-act play, *Back to Methuselah*, that was written between 1918 and 1920 and first performed in 1921. The play begins with Adam and Eve in the Garden of Eden and passes through various epochs to a final stage set in the year 31, 920 A.D. It imaginatively presents the struggles needed to put mind and body in order, as a precondition of bringing harmony into the world. The play moves into to a future in which the life span will be extended to three hundred years. By this time, carnal life would be subdued, and flesh would be displaced by a 'whirlpool of pure intelligence.' The process would not be compelled by evolution, but be one of voluntary longevity.

In the mind of Shaw, men allow themselves to give way to early death because they do not understand the great public work they could accomplish if they experienced an extended life span. In the future, men inspired by an *élan vital* or life force will live far beyond the biblical limits of three score and twenty. Good nutrition will help, but the prolongation will be essentially a matter of will-power. Deep within themselves men will come to understand that such longevity is necessary if the world is to have the good governance that is necessary for survival.[9]

Such dramatic fantasies of extraordinary longevity should be compared with a more sober understanding of how men in the later years of a normal life span can make substantial contributions to the good of society. There were many examples in the years following the Great War. During the Second World War, Winston Churchill, when in his late sixties, led Great Britain during a time of great peril, and he was an important public figure for much of the remainder of his long life. At age seventy, during the Korean

---

9. G. Bernard Shaw, *Back to Methuselah: A Metabiological Pentateuch* (Oxford: Oxford University Press, 1947). One character in the play, speaking of the extension of life to three hundred years, says that men will eventually live that long " . . . not because they would like to, but because the soul deep down in them will know that they must, if the world is to be saved." *Ibid.*, Part Two. See also Ivor Brown, *Shaw in His Time*, Ch. 7 (1965); Margery M Morgan, "Back to Methuselah, The Poet and the City," in G. B. Shaw, *A Collection of Critical Essays*. R. J. Kaufmann, Ed. (Englewood Cliffs, N.J.: Prentice Hall, 1965) 130-42.

War, Douglas MacArthur was able to persuade much younger officers of the merits of an audacious amphibious assault at Inchon. Konrad Adenauer became the oldest elected official in Western history when he became Chancellor of (West) Germany in nineteen forty-nine at age seventy four, and he held that office for fourteen years. When he was seventy-seven, Angelo Roncalli became Pope John XXIII. He brought a 'breath of newness' into that highest spiritual office, which included the convening of the progressive Second Vatican Council. In our own time, retired Senator Alan Simpson has co-chaired the important National Commission on Fiscal Responsibility and Reform; in the international realm, a global Council of Elders established by Nelson Mandela has made important contributions to general peace.

All of these achievements are in their own way remarkable, but what do they contribute to our general understanding of longevity? Usually, an individual must have had an established career in some form of public life if there are to be any expectations of further social accomplishments in later years. But that is not necessarily true. It is a principle of democracy that ordinary people can do extraordinary things, and the principle applies to every stage of life. An average individual who did not do anything of general importance during his working years can, if properly motivated, do something more than lead a stagnant life in retirement. What greater good he will do cannot be determined in advance, but such doing is a matter of practical importance. As the numbers of the older population expand, the burden of maintaining them will fall more heavily upon the younger generations. They will resent carrying that burden if the recipients feel no obligation to be socially useful.[10]

From Geriatrics to Gerontology

However else he was enlightened on the subject, Oliver Wendell Holmes shared in a traditional belief that old age was a disease. Only gradually did the medical profession at large come to

---

10. See, generally, Robert S. DeRopp, *Man Against Aging* (New York: St. Martin's Press, 1960).

understand that old age was not in itself a malady but rather a phase of life that was inherently valuable, even though subject to serious illnesses. With the founding of the specialty of geriatrics early in the twentieth century, physicians began to take a distinct interest in the pathologies of old age. The prevention and cure of illnesses that inflict those in senescence has gained in particular importance.

From a philosophical point of view, this new emphasis may be seen as a confirmation of some ancient wisdom. Many of the early thinkers in Western Civilization looked upon advanced years as liberation from physical life. They thought that at this stage of existence the soul could now really flourish, since it no longer has much to do with the body. But Aristotle taught that the body must be intact if old age is to be a time of happiness. The increased application of medical resources to the needs of the elderly in our own time can be thought of as a vindication of Aristotle's point of view.

Early medicine looked upon the health of the body in terms of the rise and fall of heat. This attitude lasted well into the nineteenth century, as was the case with Holmes's view of the body as a carbon furnace. There have also been mechanical understandings of our physical life. This approach has a spiritual analogy. Like St Paul's view of the Christian community (Rom 12), the human body has many limbs and organs that are interdependent. In more scientific terms, the body is a vast machine made up of many smaller machines.

The great advances of modern medicine have been applied with positive results for all in the period of old age. Newer forms of vaccination, drug therapy, and public health measures—such as those that lessened the dangers of tobacco—are all notable, as are the wonderful improvements in the arts of surgery. (I am myself a beneficiary of by -pass heart surgery.) The new sciences of genetics open up unlimited possibilities, as do improvements in the understanding of the interactions between mind and body. We now know that mind is not just a function of the brain; it is also subject to all the factors that influence the body. We gain in understanding of the cerebral functions while at the same time are frustrated by our inability as yet to cure its greatest malady —Alzheimer's disease.

It has been said that aging is itself a state of mind. As we become more aware of this change of life, we begin to realize that we can no longer take our physical well-being for granted. Our organs no longer take care of themselves. Geriatrics becomes, in part, self-administered. Care and prudent use must be combined in a process of prevention and individual improvement. Proper nutrition is essential. And as muscular and respiratory difficulties increase, they must be offset by aerobic exercises such as walking and swimming. Moderate weight lifting and resistance training are also desirable, since they will increase oxygen intake, should improve our general physical functioning, and may be able even to reverse feebleness.

Advances in biotechnology raise hopes for finding new cures for our many illnesses. But what if these developments could not only cure our maladies but also increase our longevity? Could the science and medicine of the twenty-first century provide us with ageless bodies? These and related questions were taken up by President George W. Bush's distinguished Council on Bioethics. In 2003, the Council, under the Chairmanship of Leon Kass of the University of Chicago, filed its report. It was titled *Beyond Therapy: Biotechnology and the Pursuit of Happiness.*

The *Beyond Therapy* report took account of the fact that the purpose of developing medical science was not only to conquer particular diseases but also to promote a process of life-extension. The aim was to increase both the average and the maximum lifespan. It is an attempt to eliminate, and not just combat, our most threatening illnesses such as cardiovascular disease, cancer, and diabetes. Many who are entering the class of the elderly look to the advancements in biotechnology to enable them to perform their existing tasks more effectively and gain a greater sense of happiness and well-being.

The hope is for an increase in the understanding of what causes the debilities of old age and improvements in the preservation of bodily health that can be secured from the abundance of nature. But taken to an extreme, biotechnology can be understood as an effort to realize an infinite prolongation of life on earth. The responsibility of the Council on Bioethics was to try to assess whether such a desire was one that was reasonable for the nation to pursue.[11]

With the passage of time, the aging process has consequences that, in their contrarian ways, struggle for predominance within the individual. There is, first, the inevitable decline of our mental and, especially, of our physical capacities. This is a frightening and inexorable process. Yet even as our bodies are diminished by the weight of years, the accumulation of experience that is made possible by improved longevity may bring us an enjoyable increase of wisdom.

In the advanced years we are also in need of refocusing our fundamental desires, since what we want begins to exceed what we can reasonably expect to accomplish. In his poem *Old Age*, Matthew Arnold noted that, as we age " . . . we feel but half, and feebly, what we feel." Discomfort with the imbalance between desire and achievement is not only frustrating; it also provides an incentive for the discovery of new means of age-retardation. As the Kass Report understands the problem, the hope for a longer and more satisfying life with less decay is a noble ambition. But if the objective is to keep people alive indefinitely, the members of the Council on Bioethics concluded that that hope is incompatible with our inescapable mortality. Ironically, there can be no going *Back To Methuselah*.[12]

The project for the prolongation of human life is in tension with the natural processes of reproduction. The demographics are alarming. Some time before the year 2030, the number of older people living on the planet will outnumber children for the first time in human history. As mortality rates improve, fertility

---

11. *Beyond Therapy: Biotechnology and the Pursuit of Happiness*, A Report of the President's Council on Bioethics (Washington & New York: The Dana Press, 2003). The Report affirms that the developments in biotechnology have not only therapeutic effects, but can also alter the powers of mind and body. It is those capacities that make biotechnology attractive to those who would like to have a younger appearance, perform better, and feel happier.

12. *Beyond Therapy*, Part IV.

declines. Many who are in their reproductive years and anticipating a long life postpone having children, often until a time when natural conception is unlikely. Meanwhile, the aging population increases. As the "baby boomers" (those born between 1946 and 1964) begin to retire, the elderly will constitute about fifteen percent of the total population. The "oldest old"—those eighty and over—have become the fastest growing sector. These generational changes have important economic consequences. With fewer young adults of working age, economic expansion becomes problematic. The amounts contributed to social security, pensions, and health premiums diminish, while the elderly continue to consume a disproportionate amount of important resources.[13]

The *Report* does not challenge the assertion of Shaler that human beings are unique because they can have a meaningful life after the reproductive years. The Council recognizes that there is a moral case to be made for living longer. If our lives are substantially extended, we can have more time to enjoy what we have built or created and also be enabled to enter into a broader conversation with society at large. If life is good, more life is, at least logically, better. Yet as life expectancy increases, the indefinite time extension can cause problems for the moral development of the individual.

Whatever goodness we attribute to a person depends to a large extent upon how well he or she honors commitments. When an individual accepts important responsibilities, there is a reasonable expectation that they can be fulfilled within what is inevitably a limited time frame. However, if we should come to believe that our future time on earth is virtually unlimited, this change of perspective can weaken our regard for outstanding duties. We may have less respect for the importance of the "here and now," which can be dangerous if the interests of those we have undertaken to care for are in jeopardy.[14]

---

13. Charles C. Mann, "The Coming Death Shortage." *The Atlantic Monthly*, May, 2005, 92-102.

14. *Beyond Therapy*, Chapter 4, IV, A 2.

The Council conceded that the advances being made in biotechnology could increase average life expectancy beyond what would otherwise be anticipated. It was now in the realm of possibility that the average life span could increase until age ninety, although the Council did point out that the maximum life span, which is now about one hundred twenty-two years, is not likely to change. Nonetheless, certain improvements in physical maintenance are encouraged to continue. Muscular enhancement and added restrictions in caloric intake are part of the progress. All of these developments will slow the degenerative process as well as affect the average life span. But these desirable improvements do not of themselves increase the overall well-being either of society as a whole or of the individual person. For it is as true now as it was in Tennyson's time that 'life piled on life / were all too little.'[15]

Our dignity calls for a fulfillment, as far as possible, of the inborn potentials that define us, both in ourselves and as participants in the human drama as a whole. A complete life is not a simple accumulation of time, nor is it one of monotonous duration. Human existence is a complex narrative composed of different stages of both development and decline. To be elderly is to be at a point in the journey that is markedly different from the periods that preceded it. When one is old, one is not the same as when one was as a middle-aged adult. An older person is now in the class of what the Spanish call *adultos mejores*—those who are, or should be, at a fuller stage of growth and maturity than at any other time. Of course, the elderly are even further removed from the confused existence of the adolescent or young adult.[16]

As the number of elderly multiplies, the gap between them and those in earlier stages of life increases. The isolation of older persons becomes more pronounced. Contemporary society tends to treat them as a separate class, who may be dealt with by pity or contempt, but rarely as persons of equal importance. Like Lear,

---

15. The reference is to Tennyson's poem *Ulysses*. See also Part V of *Beyond Therapy*.

16. Compare Gilbert Meilaender, "Thinking About Aging." *First Things*, April 2011, 37-43.

our old are unaccommodated. As they have no justifiable position in the ongoing social processes, they are usually assigned to residences composed of persons of like age and condition. There is no doubt that living in retirement communities has many positive benefits, but exclusive co-existence with one's own contemporaries can lead to a closed circle of interdependence. When left to its own devices, aging turns in upon itself in a resignation that is shadowed by despair.[17]

The humanistic challenge is to reconcile the generational differences and create a society that is welcoming to all ages. This is a profoundly complicated and arduous task. The antagonism between the extremes—those living in the final stages of life and those for whom the journey of being human is just beginning—has been one of the great laments of philosophers. Dr. Johnson thought that a harmonization between young and old was hardly possible, for you cannot unite the contrarieties of Spring and Winter. And it is true that, since the young have ideas that the old do not share, some separation is inevitable. But with good will and tenderness much of the opposition can be reduced, if not totally overcome.

Mutual understanding can grow, if the old do not try either to imitate or to compete with the young. Conversely, it is important that the young see the old as being at an ontological, as well as a chronological, distance from themselves. This is the basis of mutual respect. If the old are comfortable with their position in life, and not of a peevish disposition, the deference of the newer generations toward them may increase. In a spirit of reciprocity, they can advance each other's interests and begin to make up for each other's deficiencies. The young can learn to honor the old not just for their length of years, but, more importantly, for the quality of their character. It is important to understand that, over time, older persons will have more to contribute to the newer generations

---

17. " . . . antiquity is alien . . . and old people are a separate form of life . . . permanently other . . . ." Donald Hall, "Out the Window, the View in Winter." *The New Yorker*, January 1, 2012, 40–43.

than all who are younger than themselves can contribute to their longevity.[18]

An inclusive humanism would be one of generational amplitude. Each stage of life would have its legitimate place in the whole, and there would be meaningful exchanges across, as well as within, generations. A flexible exchange would replace mutual alienation. Those of advanced years would demonstrate, by deed as well as word, how they could contribute to a fuller life for all who are younger than they. To begin, older persons must more explicitly abide by the principles of intergenerational justice.

As the elderly live longer, the longer can be their control of essential resources. In colonial America, old men had such an extensive power over the available land that it obstructed the advancement of the young. Today, the possibilities of inordinate wealth lie more with dominance in financial investments than in real estate. It has been charged that, rather than help the young begin their own careers, the "rich oldsters" are spending their large disposable income on purely self-regarding interests. There are other complications. The author of the 1909 *Report on National Vitality* envisioned a future America where energetic elderly would continue to participate directly in the economy. The age of retirement may, of course, be raised, but when those employed can forestall retirement because of a healthy longevity, they will have little incentive to make way for those coming after them. This could lead to greater resentment by the younger members of society, and further weaken an already fragile social balance.

With respect to justice for older persons, there is a need to develop an effective consensus as to their basic entitlements. Indeed, the rights of the elderly are being addressed by the international community as well as in domestic forums. In 1991 the General Assembly of the United Nations articulated a series of principles designed to help the growing number of older persons

---

18. Samuel Johnson wrote several essays on old age. One noted that the young feel contempt for elders who try to imitate or compete with them. And the young will appreciate the wisdom of men " . . . whom they consider as placed at a distance from them in the ranks of existence." *The Rambler*, 50, September 8, 1750.

throughout the world "add life to the years that have been added to life." These principles are meant to assure the independence of the elderly through adequate access to the basic material necessities of life as well as health care and education. The aim is that willing and capable older persons will be enabled to make a contribution to the ongoing social life of their communities. This can be by way of volunteerism as well as employment, and the United Nations Declaration emphasizes that the social involvement of the elderly should be without regard to their economic contribution.

Participation is meant primarily to ensure that those of advanced age have a voice in the formulation of all the policies that affect them, and also make it possible for them to share their knowledge and skills with all the members of society. Postponing the age of retirement may be an economic necessity. Yet it should be remembered that no matter how extensively older persons are enabled to participate in the ongoing works of society, they must not become too deeply involved in matters of immediate concern. For if older persons are to pass on their gifts of wisdom and experience to succeeding generations, they must maintain some distance from the frenzy of daily strife and competition.[19]

Old age brings the whole of life into perspective. Such broad comprehension is valuable not only to the elderly themselves, but also to those who are gradually succeeding them. Unfortunately, much of this accumulated wisdom is not being passed on. The general population is too busy with the present to understand the significance of the past or to anticipate what may come in the future. Nonetheless, a more open and generous exchange among those in the various stages of life can lead to great improvements in the well-being of all. In the contemporary world it is the responsibility of older persons to help the rest of human beings become aware of themselves and see how much they are missing of a more complete human existence. Those of advanced years know better than others the range, as well as the limits, of self-sufficiency. Not

---

19. Kinsella, Kevin, & Wan He *An Aging World,* 2008. (Washington, DC: US Census Bureau, 2009). See also United Nations General Assembly Resolution 46/91, 16 December 1991.

only do they have more experience; they are also detached from the anxious hurriedness of modern life and its pervasive immaturities.

There is a well-established tradition that encourages grandparents to have a formative influence upon their grandchildren. .But it is much harder for older persons to extend the realm of their authority to those of more proximate status. Those who are young adults, or of middle age, are much more difficult to reach by way of advice and admonition. Those who have passed adolescence are either too caught up in making their own way, or, if they have had success, satisfied with just enjoying whatever it is that they have already accomplished. They are thus insulated from the reflective understanding of those further along on the course of life. Fearful of old age, they rationalize their apprehension by assuming that the interests of older persons are essentially different from their own.

Better connections between older persons and other adults may be developed if it is acknowledged that those who are caught up in the demands of ongoing life have inherited a society passed on to them by their seniors. Those now in the final stages of life are in many ways responsible for the existing state of affairs. Seniors may wish to congratulate themselves on how much they have contributed to the development of the American technological colossus and to the dominant materialism, but they must also be willing to recognize what they did wrong and not just take credit for what they did right. The most important contribution that older persons can make to the broader human community is to retrospectively examine their lives, and then acknowledge and, as far as possible, correct their mistakes. In doing so, they can arrive at a better understanding of the overall value of their lives and thus be enabled to make constructive contributions to the progress of their broader communities.

Having reached retirement, older persons can see things more clearly than in earlier stages of life, when their minds were clouded by passion and ambition. They are now able to understand how much that they had believed desirable is in fact unjust or inhuman. And, if they possess any moral authority, they will give voice to their dissent. For who, in this terminal period of life, can honestly believe that a culture of consumerism should be the exclusive, or even the primary, purpose of living? Or, that living to work rather than working to live should be the standard? Yet these are the reigning ideologies. The tragedy is that those for whom this is an acceptable way of life fail to see how much of it constitutes a diminishment of their human nature.

A long childhood followed by an extended old age seems to be the course that the human race is taking in this third millennium. However, those who now constitute the older generation are able to see that adolescence can last too long and that many who qualify as adults have never really grown up. They may have taken on important responsibilities, such as starting and raising a family, but tenacious immaturities still impede their development. The deeper deficiencies appear in middle age. Between forty and sixty-five, a certain physical deterioration begins, but there is little mental or spiritual improvement. An incapacity to distinguish what is banal from what is serious remains an impediment to growth, and a sense of playfulness, so important to a full life, often collapses into an obsession with organized sports. The possibilities of pleasurable enjoyment are narrowed by the eroticism and love of violence that began poisoning their lives when they were younger. Many of those living out this interim period have little comprehension of higher delights nor are they prone to the discipline of reflective thought. Political engagement, if it exists at all, is primarily emotive rather than rational. Moreover, the comforts and gratifications available in the private realm tend to cancel all broader social perspectives. George Bernard Shaw is not the only one to recognize the depths of modern immaturity and its effects upon the general tone of society as well as the quality of governance.

Much of this unadultness has been going on for a very long time, and those now seniors must acknowledge how much they have contributed to this sorry state of affairs. At an earlier age, those now old were too compliant. The prevailing way of life enabled them to climb the ladder of financial and social success and, in most cases, to properly raise their families. Yet they vaguely realized that, in spite of its positive features, the conventional way of life was impeding a deeper development of their personalities. What was lacking was the courage to challenge the pervasive possessiveness of the consumer society. Now, as older persons, they can put much of that behind them. In spite of physical infirmities, they can become more mature with respect to mind and spirit. They can also initiate a humanistic dialogue about the quality of our culture. They can raise questions about what it means to be fully human in conversations not just among themselves, but also with those who will eventually succeed them. If those of middle age are willing to accept the challenge of reconstruction, they can grow into a more authentic state of maturity. By activating their dormant powers of thought and feeling, they can begin to understand more of what it means to live well rather than to just exist.

Such a dialogue between old persons and those in middle age can bring the different generations closer together in pursuit of a greater dignity for all. As things now stand, society caters to the young. But youth is too busy with itself and with its technological gadgets to make a lasting contribution to social development. At the other extreme, older persons have lost the capacity to have a direct influence upon human progress. The directing of the major instruments of common life into a more fully human condition is primarily the responsibility of those of middle age.

The control of the major instruments of society is in the hands of those who have passed young adulthood and reached a certain level of maturity. If these persons wish to improve the media, the economy, and the general culture, they should look towards those ahead of them in the development of life for advice and guidance. In such a broader interaction the generations, which seem to simply supplant one another over time, will, in important ways, begin to live together in terms of shared values. The lives of older persons and those of middle age will overlap as they try to make modern society more compatible with human dignity. These conversations will also elevate the aspirations of the young. As the extremes of life are reconciled, there will be a new harmony in which the various stages of being human begin to complement each other. A society will begin to emerge that is welcoming to all.

Advanced Old Age

As we take greater account of the psychological and social consequences of aging, we move beyond the specialty of geriatrics and enter the broader field of gerontology, where all the various aspects of senescence are brought together in order to understand the process as a whole. Nevertheless, the bodily dimension has a certain primacy. Even with the advances in biotechnology, modern medicine does not seek to extend life into an endless future. Its more modest aim is to try to keep all of our physical systems going together for approximately the same length of time, while avoiding long periods of disability or sudden mortality. Eventually, all the organs would shut down more or less simultaneously. This is called compression of morbidity. As a limited form of life-extension, it is considered to be achievable through the combined efforts of the physician and the patient who, in his or her daily life, follows the doctor's advice on exercise, nutrition, and medication. Considered imaginatively, this scenario can be likened to Holmes's poem "The One-Horse Shay," where there is a " . . . breakdown all at once, and nothing first/ Just as bubbles do as when they burst." However, even as we anticipate longer periods of life for most of the elderly, we must take full account of the extent of longevity in this modern age.[20]

Many of the reflections that we have already considered distinguish old age as such from a further indeterminate period of decrepitude. Today, we make a distinction between the old and the very old—between those who are growing old in a relatively healthy condition and the less visible "old old," those who, while living long, must endure increasing incapacities. Modern medicine has made it possible for the elderly to make real improvements in

---

20. According to the President's Council on Bioethics, " . . . All the scenarios for happy life extension depend on technologies that will keep all the body's systems going for roughly the same duration, after which time they will shut down more or less simultaneously. . . . "*Beyond Therapy,* 207.

their lives after age sixty-five; however, in the late seventies and beyond, a more restrictive and disabling stage begins. It has been predicted that by the middle of this century the number of those above age eighty-five will increase four-fold. It is important that we have a realistic understanding of these changes.[21]

Will those who last to an advanced old age be living too long to live well? That is the central question. When mobility is impaired and infirmities multiply, there is a loss of independence as well as an increase in suffering, and dependency does not fit well with our ideals of autonomy. Those who are experiencing the loss of liberty find it difficult to attribute a continuing purpose to their lives. It becomes harder for them to believe that their being alive makes any real difference in the lives of others.

The very old have lost " . . . an audience and a secular station." They fear that those who bother to visit will be coming not because they really want to see them, but rather merely with the intention of fulfilling a moral duty. As their numbers and disabilities increase they are in danger of becoming a truly lost generation.[22]

In advanced senescence many of the moral failings traditionally associated with old age begin to intensify. The extremely old are more likely to be subject to depression, to fall into deeper self-centeredness, and to cultivate a peevish attitude towards the entire world around them. They are increasingly isolated no matter where they reside, developing resentments, exaggerating their infirmities, and becoming more demanding. The boredom that hovers over every aspect of old age can become pervasive. And all these difficulties are more likely to be suffered by women than by men, since women make up two-thirds of the older old, and also constitute eighty-five percent of our centenarians.[23]

---

21. Vienna International Plan of Action on Aging (New York: United Nations, 1983).

22. The quotation is from Auden's poem "On Visiting an Old Person's Home."

23. Susan Jacoby, *Never Say Die: The Myth and Marketing of the New Old Age* (New York: Pantheon Books, 2011).

Two basic problems are the worsening of health over time and, for all but the very rich, the increasing menace of poverty. The promise of an ever-extending life span that was to come from the benevolence of biotechnology loses its allure, as the more important needs of care and maintenance come into prominence. Fantasies of never-ending life begin to dissolve. It becomes obvious that resources that could be expended upon geriatric research need to be applied to social services that could enable the very old to live a more dignified life. But the fundamental problem is the more personal one of increasing isolation and a deepening loneliness. When these of advanced years become extremely infirm, they are often transferred to institutional care. In his poem *Old People's Home* Auden imaginatively captures the experience of these lost souls fading away " . . . not at home but assigned/ to a frequent numbered ward, stowed out of conscience/ as unpopular luggage."

In spite of these hardships, we should never forget that every stage of human life has an inherent dignity. A very old age—of either a man or a woman—must be respected by all, and especially by those who, like themselves, belong to the category of seniors. Age discrimination is usually imposed by society upon the elderly. However, those at earlier stages of old age are often indifferent towards the most vulnerable members of their own community. We need to remember that the very old are entitled to affirmation, care, and friendship from those with whom they have a close affinity; a concern that cannot be limited to the members of one's immediate family. It is a call to the conscience of all those elderly who are not yet 'very old.'

The human suffering experienced by those who are infirm and very old cries out for a high degree of compassion, which is often not forthcoming, for reasons that are both social and personal in nature. Modern society is in constant denial of death. Consequently, it keeps out of mind those who are in a terminal condition. We all have difficulty accepting the extremes of decline as part of the common human state. Yet the degree to which we accept or reject the last stages of life on earth determines the quality of our personal character and of our civilization: As Pope Benedict has observed:

> The true meaning of humanity is essentially determined in relation to suffering and to the sufferer. This holds true both for the individual and for society. A society unable to accept its suffering members and incapable of helping to share their suffering and to bear it inwardly through 'com-passion' is a cruel and inhuman society.[24]

The very old who are suffering, either at home or in a nursing facility, have special need for compassion. Their material essentials must be met and forms of socialization and education generously extended to them. But beyond these fundamentals there is a more basic desire that is too often ignored. For more than anything else, the very old yearn for some form of authentic interpersonal contact with others who are sympathetic to their plight. Here Martin Buber's famous aphorism—to be alive is to be spoken to—has a special poignancy. A visit and some conversation—however brief—can be an expression of a singular compassion. Such meetings can be reciprocally beneficial. The ones addressed are lifted up from their isolation and have the satisfaction of express recognition of their continuing membership in the human community. The visitors are also enriched. The encounter can have the quality of a shared suffering. By identifying with the other's suffering, the visitors have made it a part of their own inner being. There is a growth in love and maturity. In terms of Christian fellowship the encounter has knitted together two otherwise lonely hearts and directs them both, in a vision of hope, toward a happiness that lies ahead and beyond the miseries of advanced human life.

Since those who are older longer can be greatly infirm in both mind and body, it is sometimes suggested that in such a state they are no longer the persons that they once were. Negative metaphors

---

24. Pope Benedict XVI, Encyclical Letter, *Saved in Hope (Spe Salvi)*, 38 (2007). The Holy Father insists that the compassionate initiatives must come from individuals, rather than societies as such, and that "the individual cannot accept another's suffering unless he personally is able to find meaning in suffering, a path of purification and growth in maturity, a journey of hope...."

are often crudely and cruelly used to describe their condition, and such descriptions are often followed by appeals to physician-assisted suicide. Yet no matter how great their infirmities, these weakened individuals retain their human dignity. Their personalities may have gone into some form of remission, but they can also be wonderfully drawn out if only they are given some time and attention.

Recently I visited a man who was a family friend and was himself celebrating his ninety-ninth birthday. He was confined to a wheelchair, his appearance was disheveled, and during our meeting his mind often wandered incoherently. But once he made contact and realized who I was, he became animated. He spoke with fond memories of the years gone by and also generously inquired as to my well-being. In spite of the decline of both mind and body, there was no doubt that the individual whom I had known for years was still there. In visiting him I received as much as I gave.

Old age is a time of mutual neediness. Those who are in relatively good health must learn the lessons of caring by moving beyond their own comforts and widening the scope of their concerns. Family is, of course, of paramount importance, but we must also broaden our concept of those for whom we bear some responsibility. The need for the care of the very old is increasing at a time when family ties have weakened and the number of volunteer caregivers has declined. As a young American philosopher has observed, " . . . we live in a world in which the Sisters of Mercy have just about disappeared."[25] We must take up the slack.

---

25. Peter Lauler, *The New Atlantis*, 3-13 (2005).

3

The Quest for Maturity

Introduction

Let us begin by reviewing some of the principal ideas about the nature and meaning of Old Age that we have already considered. In the first chapter, titled *Old Age through the Ages,* we saw how some of the philosophers of the Ancient Worlds of Greece and Rome applied their speculative powers to the subject of old age. This was the time of some of the greatest thinkers in the Western Tradition: Plato and Aristotle, Cicero and Seneca. They all thought that humans were, by nature, rational animals composed of both body and soul. They also recognized that, with the onset of old age, physical powers decline. But this was not for them an unmitigated disaster, for they believed that the powers of soul and mind are elevated even as the body deteriorates. For these thinkers, the elderly had more intangible pleasures available to them than they had earlier in their lives. Their understanding was now less a function of their senses and more a matter of the mind. Old age was also advantageous because it was a time for the forming of associations and companionships no longer entangled in the passions of lust, ambition, and rivalry. Opportunities for convivial meals and conversations with others were thought of as a primary source of blessing. And at least for some, like Cicero, older persons could still make important contributions to society, even though what they were able to do was more limited and deliberative than the impulsive and energetic actions of the young.[1]

---

1. See authorities cited in Chapter One.

The Quest for Maturity

The quality of old age was considered to be a consequence of the time that preceded it. The choices we made in the past have brought us to who we are now in the advanced years of human life. If individuals now elderly had been intemperate and imprudent in their younger years, the later years would register the deficits. However, if they had led a morally sound life, a pleasant old age could be expected. Beyond that, in the literature of the Ancient World not much was said about the capacity of the old to grow further in matters of moral virtue.

By the time of the medieval period, the culture of the West had moved from a pagan to a Christian, worldview. The realities of human depravity and decay were more fully understood; indeed, in official church teaching these deficiencies were given great emphasis. But during this period there were also within this religious culture aspirations for spiritual growth that reached every stage of life. A clearer grasp of the ultimate purposes of being human encouraged the pursuit of higher virtues even by those of advanced years. This change was reflected in Dante's *Banquet*. There the great poet imagined the elderly as having a fuller understanding of the principles of justice, as being wiser and more prudential in their judgments, and as having a magnanimous attitude towards those younger than themselves. Unfortunately, these ideals found little confirmation in actual experience. During the Middle Ages old age was rarely considered as an accomplishment, and a class of old people as such did not exist. Those who lived long lives were few, and, unless they were in the class of warriors or of the nobility, they had little status.[2]

These were turbulent times, when the strengths of the young were indispensable to survival. Since the old were not active agents of history, few took the time to understand them as they really were. By the time of the Renaissance, whatever authority an elderly man or woman commanded was generally limited to a superior position within the family. Outside such intimate circles, they were odious. As the general society progressed in refinement, the

---

2. Simone de Beauvoir, *The Coming of Age,* Trans. Patrick O'Brien (New York: G. P. Putnam, 1972).

physical frailties of aging became even more obvious. If not subject to ridicule, old people were seen as pitiable. As Shakespeare described it, old age meant the loss of much of what we consider to be at least physically essential to a normal human life. A conviction was developing that when we age we lose all of what makes life worth living.

With the beginning of the modern world there was some restatement of the powers of old age. Goethe lived into his eighties. He used his longevity for a fuller unfolding of his inward powers and a broadening of his comprehension of the world in which he lived. During this period there was also a reconsideration of the traditional questions concerning the relationships between the young and the old. Samuel Johnson saw little prospect of closer encounters between those launching their lives and those winding them down, but he thought that some honoring of the elderly by the young was possible so long as the objective distances of being and experience between them were realistically acknowledged.[3]

Dr. Johnson also addressed the subject of retirement. He thought that an elderly man should freely accept that status, as otherwise he would be compelled to relinquish his employment. Family support was essential, because without it being unemployed would lead to neglect and contempt from the broader society. Whatever happiness could be found in this state of idleness would come from the unselfish devotion to meaningful causes or relationships. A deeper religious piety was also advisable, given the proximity of death and judgment.

Throughout this period, while institutional support of the elderly increased, the results were not encouraging. With little to stimulate their minds or their interests, those residing in such confining circumstances tended to reduce their desires to the fundamentals of existence. Too often they abandoned all hope for a satisfactory old age. The sense of their uselessness grew in the

---

3. According to Johnson, we can never unite the "contraries of Spring and Winter"; it is unjust to claim the privileges of age and retain the playthings of childhood. Yet, " . . . the young always form magnificent ideas of the wisdom and gravity of men whom they consider as placed at a distance from them in the ranks of existence . . . ." (*The Rambler*, #50, September 8, 1750).

minds of others as well. In an imaginative novel, Anthony Trollope envisioned a time of forced retirement of the elderly by government decree followed, after a period of reflection, with a humane form of euthanasia.[4]

In the advancing Victorian culture the public accomplishments of older persons were celebrated, but in the world of letters the appraisal was mixed. Browning would claim that "the best was yet to be," and Tennyson was sure that "some work of noble note" could still be achieved, but Matthew Arnold was equally certain that growing old meant a loss of feeling as well as all powers for meaningful action. For Arnold, rather than a mellowing of life into a golden age, the old would find themselves suffering "month by month with weary pain."[5]

At the start of our own American history, the elderly had a favorable social position. This was due primarily to the fact that the early settlers were a deeply religious people who incorporated biblical principles of respect for the aged into their basic social fabric. Old age was both venerable and godly, and this elevated status was expressed in power. Older men held positions of authority in both Church and State, and they controlled much of the new country's primary asset—land.

The Hebrew Scriptures were particularly valuable during the Colonial period, because not only did they confer status upon the elderly, but they also established standards of conduct that were applicable to the old as well as to the young. In the Massachusetts Bay Colony the aged were criticized as well as appreciated. And the young who felt that their ambitions were being unfairly limited by the economic and social dominance of the old also expressed their own displeasure. With the Revolution and the Declaration of Independence, the standard of equality gained a new prominence that called into question all disparities of power. The moral authority of the elders began to go into decline, and expressions of disrespect gained greater circulation.

4. Anthony Trollope, *The Fixed Period* (1882) (Penguin edition, 1993).
5. Arnold's poem *Growing Old* was published in 1867, when Arnold was forty-five years old. He died in 1888.

Reflections On Old Age

The New England Renaissance of the early nineteenth century brought a flourishing of art and thought that was, on the whole, favorably inclined towards the old. Although Thoreau had said that he had never learned anything important from older men, Ralph Waldo Emerson and Oliver Wendell Holmes knew better. They had both read Cicero's classic on the subject, and each in his own way realized that the thought of the Roman master could be restated to the advantage of their own time.

Emerson dismissed the adverse opinion of the vulgar crowd towards the elderly because it was based on external appearances. The real strength of age was inward. Like Cicero, Emerson realized the authority of old age rested upon the invisible powers of mind and imagination. Old people were noble to the degree that they did not fear the opinions of ordinary society. The elderly had no anxieties here, as long as their reputations were already well established. Where their deeds were great, they had already contributed to the growth of civilization. Moreover, if their minds were not impaired, they were resourceful. For Emerson, one of the intangible advantages of age was that people living a longer life were able to unify disparate thoughts and bring their unfinished intellectual projects to completion. Emerson also knew that one who loves is never really old.[6]

As a descriptive writer, Holmes accurately recorded how the elderly appeared to others when walking on the streets of Cambridge and Boston. As a physician, he was able to recommend various forms of exercise that could help them sustain their bodily constitutions in the later years. At the same time, Holmes had some critical opinions of the elderly. The most serious was directed at the tendency of old people to allow fixed habits to control their future actions. Such rigidity in the face of contingencies impaired the power of self-determination that to Holmes was of paramount value.[7]

---

6. Ralph Waldo Emerson, "Old Age," in *The Works of Ralph Waldo Emerson*, Vol. 7 *(Society and Solitude)*, Fireside Edition (New York, 1909).

7. Oliver Wendell Holmes, *The Autocrat of the Breakfast-Table* (1882), Chapter VII (A Common Reader ed., 2001). Holmes, who lived for 86 years, was a physician, writer, and father of the famous Supreme Court Justice Oliver Wendell Holmes, Jr. The senior Holmes believed that "habit is a confession

Other positive evaluations came out of this New England revival, even as it remained realistic about the nature of old age. Longfellow, for one, had some encouraging verses. In a poem he had written for his college reunion, Longfellow stated with confidence that, even as we age, "something remains for us to do or dare / even the oldest tree some fruit may bear." But like the earlier periods of Western history, the culture of New England had negative as well as positive appraisals of this last stage of life on earth. A poem written in the Colonial period by Anne Bradstreet seemed more relevant to the changing status of the old in the new, post-civil war economy. She had described the elderly person as one who understood that "... hands and arms, once strong, had lost their might / I cannot labor, nor can I fight." With the rise of industrialization in the latter part of the nineteenth century, it was that loss of physical strength that was making older people obsolete.[8]

The seeming irrelevance of the aged to modern social prosperity had early precedents. Recall how in the sixteenth century the French writer Michel de Montaigne wrote an essay on old age in which he explored the relative position of young and old in the period roughly between the Middle Ages and the beginning of the modern world. At that time, one rarely lived to an extended old age. Many remained working as craftsmen or peasant farmers up until the time of their deaths in their late thirties or early forties. This meant that the young had fewer opportunities. Montaigne thought that the situation was not only socially unjust; it was also an affront to human nature. He thought that our souls "were as developed at twenty as they are ever to be," so that the disproportion of employment opportunities quashed some of the most creative spirits. Those surviving past thirty held all the available jobs, but they had little to contribute to the well-being of the social whole.[9]

---

of failure in the highest function of being, which involves a perpetual self-determination, in full view of all existing circumstances...." (155).

8. Longfellow's poem is *Morituri Salutamus*, which he delivered at his fiftieth college reunion in 1875. Born in England in 1612, Bradstreet came to America with her father aboard *The Arabella*. The comments on Old Age are part of a longer poem on the Ages of Man.

9. Michel de Montaigne (1533-1592), *Essays* (No. 57, "Of Age").

Montaigne's idea that old age was an obstacle to progress found an echo in the developing economies. Industrial production, manufacture, and transportation were becoming the main occupations, at least in the urban centers. To fill them required muscular power, speed, and efficiency. As older people lacked most of these abilities, they were being pressured to step aside and leave the field to the young. To be, or at least look and behave, young, was becoming a new measure of personal success. Yet the paradox was that, even as seniors were becoming obsolete, there were more of them, and they were living longer.

As we saw in the preceding chapter, at the beginning of the twentieth century there were some hopes that an increased longevity could pay economic dividends for the whole society. General expectations that one could live well while living old were widespread. Within the field of medicine, geriatrics became a specialty. Great advances were made in prevention and cure of the illnesses that especially inflict the aged. The science of gerontology developed as the study of the aging process in and of itself. Following the Second World War, biotechnology started to make its unique contributions to the expectations of longevity.

The maintenance of good health had become a critical part of rising hopes for an extended life. But a new emphasis was given to the prevention of aging along with the curing of its illnesses. As the report *Beyond Therapy* noted, the hope for a longer life span was a matter of mixed blessings. If life is good, more life is intuitively desirable. However, expectations of living indefinitely could endanger the performance of important responsibilities. Furthermore, the postponement or denial of reproduction was having alarming demographic and economic consequences. A disproportionate number of the elderly were using up many social resources, while at the same time the number of new births was falling. All these changes were provoking reflection upon the meaning of old age and the constituents of a full and complete human life.[10]

---

10. *Beyond Therapy: Biotechnology and the Pursuit of Happiness*. A Report of The President's Council on Bioethics (Washington and New York: The Dana Press, 2003). See also the discussion in Chapter Two of the present work.

The Quest for Maturity

Yet in spite of the difficulties, old age was beginning to be appreciated as a distinctive phase in the human life span. Retirement by age sixty-five became the standard. By the beginning of the present century, social security, pensions, and other investment plans made it possible for millions over 65 to lead relatively independent lives and look forward to many more years. These developments raised the important question of what is needed, beyond reasonably good health, to make this prolonged life span one that is both happy and fulfilling.

One helpful sign was the emergence of serious reflections upon the meaning of old age. These stressed the fact that elderly persons have, because of their experience, a more comprehensive understanding of the human condition. To make this increased wisdom of general benefit, it was necessary to reconnect those in the condition of retirement to the broader society. Greater attention was also given to some of the distinctive and positive qualities of advanced life. Some observers took notice of how, as one grows old, a contemplation of the beauties of nature gradually replaced a thirst for physical activities. The need for intellectual growth as well as physical hygiene was emphasized, as well as an insistence upon maintaining, as far as possible, a spirit of self-reliance. The possibilities inherent in the increase in the available number of years led to some changes in fundamentals. It was considered important to replace the traditional idea of old age as a time of rest with the possibility of a new sense of exploration. As Oliver Wendell Holmes had observed: " . . . to reach the port of heaven, we must sail sometimes with the wind and sometimes against it,—but we must sail, and not drift or be at anchor . . . ."[11]

Throughout the twentieth century the perennial gap between age and youth was reconsidered. It was acknowledged that women have a special talent for promoting reconciliation, but the relationships among all the living generations had to be taken into account. The stages of human life are not just times of succession. It was recognized that those past youth begin to make over the world they have inherited, while those from the mid-forties to the

11. See note vii, supra.

early sixties begin to direct, govern, and defend the established culture. Like youth, old age was traditionally thought to have no direct influence upon the course of social development. But as the elderly increased in numbers, their influence upon the other stages of life could no longer be ignored.

Older persons can treasure their accomplishments from an earlier time. But they are also aware of the mistakes they made in building up their society—mistakes that are being at least indirectly confirmed by those now in dominant positions in the economy, politics, and the general culture. It is, therefore, important that those now old not be in contact just with youth, but that they also institute a broader dialogue with those of middle age. There needs to be a conversation about stability and change among all the living generations. Older persons need to be in communication with those who, while thought to be of mature age, suffer from that pervasive immaturity that characterizes every aspect of modern life.

In more personal terms, a paramount objective of this final form of life is to reach a greater degree of harmony with ourselves and with our changing circumstances. This requires a certain degree of acceptance. We must be reconciled to the fact that there is no further stage of life to which we may look forward, nor is there any going back to an earlier, more vigorous, period. Life now has boundaries; it was not too long ago that we thought it was limitless. We must also learn to live with uncertainties, even though some may have terminal implications. As a wit once remarked, old age is a vast stage that has many trapdoors, and we never know when one of them will spring open.[12]

We have had enough experience of aging to realize that Browning's optimistic poetry is an imaginative exaggeration. But it would also be a mistake to believe that after seventy it is all downhill. We should affirm Cicero's conviction that old age is an important part of the natural order of human existence and respond accordingly. We are entering a new developmental stage of

12. Sherwin B. Nuland, *The Art of Aging* (New York, NY: Random House Trade Paperbacks, 2007).

life. Some decline is inevitable, but there can be also growth. We would do well to remember that it is best that we not think too much in terms of repose. It is better to imagine our having reached a new landfall that has many opportunities if we are willing to look for them. Such willingness to explore depends greatly upon our circumstances, both social and individual. But, most of all, it is a matter of the fundamental orientation of our personalities.[13]

Too much of what we think of ourselves has been shaped by the conventions and mores of our surrounding society. The culture celebrates celebrity, and any renown we once had is now gone. There is also the widespread belief that we are what we own, or what we do. Since most of us have limited resources and are no longer employed, our socially constructed self-image becomes increasingly irrelevant. Old age becomes the time when we are destined to discover who we are within ourselves.

The fear is that there will be nothing there to find. What are we, or what can we become, when all else that was once important to our self-esteem is gone? We have our memories, which in some degree are supportive, but too many recollections stimulate regret. If we rethink everything that we did, or failed to do, we are opening a door to depression. Better to think of ourselves as we are in our present condition. We may find, to our surprise, some substance to our otherwise impoverished being.[14]

Finding Ourselves

Self-discovery is difficult at any stage of life, and it is especially hard to establish a personal identity once we have passed into old age. We can identify ourselves with our past, but too much looking backward is dangerous, even if it involves pleasant memories. If we constantly recall happier times, we can distract our attention

---

13. G. Stanley Hall, *Senescence, The Last Half of Life* (New York, NY: D. Appleton & Company, 1922). See also Paul Tournier, *Learn to Grow Old* (Louisville, KY: Westminster/John Knox Press, 1972).

14. Joan D. Chittister, *The Gift of Years: Growing Old Gracefully* (New York: Blue Ridge, 2008).

from the pleasures that are at hand. The complete life lies ahead, not behind us. Our objective should be to bring what is of value from time past into time present and then direct ourselves towards the future. To understand who we are, we must take account of our experiences as a whole. Despite mistakes and disappointments, we have most likely formed our personalities in a manner that we can, with few reservations, affirm. And now we must go forward. As Newman observed, to live is to change, and to change often is to become perfect.

Continuing to build ourselves up as we are, we will escape from becoming what we fear. We can also experience a higher sense of freedom. In old age we become liberated from the socially constructed identities that once directed our lives. It is a great relief to realize that roles or connections no longer determine our personal value. In addition, we are free of the stagecraft that goes with all prestigious occupations. While not contemptuous of society's opinions, we are indifferent to its judgments—and its prejudices. We are also becoming more content with less. We become more unscheduled—in spite of an increase in medical appointments! Day by day we become more aware of the mystery of life, of how in this new stage of the human experience many good things can come with greater patience and an open heart.

Is there an art to aging that might apply to all of us? For starters we should remember that the admonition to "act your age" means more than avoiding foolishness. It means becoming daily more and more of an authentic adult, while at the same time retaining the playfulness that once defined our youth. Traditional virtues are given new expression. A refined prudence comes into play. Mature aging demands that we should not try to do what we know is unmanageable or beyond our mental or bodily powers. We also need to remember that the organs of our bodies work better when we pay attention to them. A healthy body is one that is still in use, even if its functions and powers have been reduced. Everything will work better if we remain conscious of the interaction between the biochemistry of our bodies and the state of our minds.

The Quest for Maturity

We should live in harmony with our environment. Women perhaps know more intuitively than men that the quality of our domestic arrangements has a great deal to do with our personal happiness. We can find peace of mind in well-arranged ordinary things and in the rhythms of daily life. Attending to what is near at hand, we can make for ourselves a surrounding shelter that is both tranquil and familiar. These adjustments that we make to our practical circumstances are of themselves to our good, yet we should not forget that such stabilities also have an instrumental purpose. They make possible the cultivation, as well as the preservation, of our individual personalities. In that respect we cannot forget that we are composed of *both* body and soul, and that the potential for individual development begins with the physical dimensions of our lives.

From a sixteenth-century treatise we have received the advice that the possibilities of a long life are centered on the virtue of temperance. Simplicity of diet is of great importance; in that regard, gluttony is a major vice that the elderly must take special care to avoid. Open air, light exercise, and "little care" also contribute to the preservation of life in a healthy way. But since ancient times it has been recommended that, as the passions subside, we should be opening our hearts and minds to the delights of reason and the pleasures of intuition. Thus we move toward what is more spiritual than physical in the core of our being.[15]

There are subtle adjustments by the way of rejuvenation. By the time we become "senior citizens" we begin to realize that the achievements of our past were at some variance with who we really are. Such accomplishments, however well deserved, were primarily an expression of our will power. They required so much single-mindedness that many aspects of our deeper and broader

---

15. Luigi Cornaro, *The Art of Living Long* (Milwaukee, WI: William F. Butler, 1916). Cornaro was a Venetian centenarian. To his mind, temperance was the supreme practical virtue: " . . . That which I call temperance is a regular and simple diet, limited by every man's experience of his own easy digestion, and thereby proportioning, as near as well can be, the daily repairs to the daily decays of our wasting bodies . . . ." *The Art of Living Long*, 146.

identities were repressed or neglected. Consequently, there was a diminishment of our personalities, which needs to be recovered.

Tennyson's call to the aged to be "strong in will" may have some continuing relevance, but there are other admonitions that are better suited to our new condition. Here it was Emerson who had the deeper understanding. While conceding that meeting the demands of life required a concentration of the will, he insisted that such volitional energy could not establish our true identities. Who we really are is more likely to be discovered through reflection than by action. This conscious cultivation of our minds, long delayed by more pressing practical concerns, can flourish only in our later years.[16]

A move towards thought is not meant to imply that the will has no role to play in old age. To act effectively at any time of life requires volition. But in advanced years the power of the will is not directly expressed in frantic activity or by intense immersion in particulars. Rather, now the primary purpose of the will is to give our lives some meaningful and overall purpose. This positive orientation serves as an antidote to stagnation. As Jung observed, in old age the will provides us with the value of a directed life.[17]

The point is to disprove Montaigne's contention that the mind is as fully developed in our twenties as it is ever to be. If in our advanced years we now really set sail, rather than drift with the tides, we can recover latent powers of the intellect and imagination that our obsession with pragmatic concerns had previously led us to ignore. We now can, like Goethe, begin to unfold the deepest aspects of our being. Our souls turn outward as well as inward. With the proper use of our reflective abilities we can begin to comprehend the greater expanse of the world that we inhabit. We can contemplate the natural beauty of our planet and the wonders of the cosmos revealed to us by the progress of the physical sciences.

16. I discuss this aspect of Emerson's personality in my study, *Person and Society in American Thought* (New York: Peter Lang, 2007), Chapter One.

17. As a physician, Jung believed that " . . . a directed life is in general better, richer, and healthier than an aimless one, and that it is better to go forward with the stream of time than backwards against it. " C. G. Jung, *Modern Man in Search of a Soul* (1933), Chapter 5, 112.

And by studying the history of our species we begin to have a fuller understanding of what it means to be a human being.

It has been said that the evening years of life cannot be ruled by the principles of the afternoon .The common understanding of the metaphor underlines the limitations and contractions of old age However, as we become older persons we can also progress, especially in matters of the mind and spirit. Our understanding of the true, the good, and the beautiful—the transcendentals of existence—can increase immeasurably. We can now more fully appreciate the fundamentals of being that we ignored when we were caught up in the busyness of life.[18]

Lifetime learning renews the soul, a fact that many colleges and universities are now addressing by offering academic courses for seniors. Here as elsewhere our earlier experiences affect the quality of later life. When we were young, educational degrees emphasized preparation for some specific task or professional or business career. If the humanities were part of those courses of study, some foundations were laid that could be built up throughout our adult lives and greatly increased after we leave active employment. If our earlier training was essentially vocational (no matter how it was labeled), growth of the intellect in old age will be more difficult, but certainly not impossible.

One of the paramount anxieties among the elderly is a fear of mental collapse into some form of dementia. Senility is a result of many factors, among which is a prolonged lack of mental activity. How can that be avoided? Some stimulation can be provided by television. This is, however, generally a poor source of enlightenment, for it is essentially a commercial medium occasionally offering, between advertisements, programs that are banal or worse. There are few sights more pitiable than the one of elderly individuals staring blankly at what is directed at them from a sterile

---

18. . . . "The afternoon of life must have a significance of its own and cannot be merely a pitiful appendage to life's meaning." Jung, op.cit., 109. For the metaphysical discussions here and following I draw heavily upon the work of Jacques Maritain, especially his seminal study, *The Degrees of Knowledge* (1932), trans. Gerald B. Phelan (South Bend, IN: University of Notre Dame Press, 1995).

screen. Some improvement of mind may be derived from reading magazines and newspapers, especially the better ones, but many of those easily available are too devoted to scandal, crime, and disaster to be a real source of pleasure and happiness. With relentless reminders of danger and tragedy, the mass media are designed to keep people on edge so that they will be satisfied with the status of being consumers. The elderly, with much time on their hands, are often the victims of such manipulation.

Where there is no intellectual or spiritual stimulation, older persons fall into a paralysis of the soul that matches the decline of their bodies. Personal sloth is partially to blame, but much more culpable is the widespread social prejudice that, with age, the human brain necessarily undergoes the same shrinkage as the body. This is quite wrong. Neurological research establishes that, while the brains of older persons are physically reduced, they nevertheless retain an intellectual competence that can continue to be developed.

Despite physical decline and suffering, it remains within the possibilities of older persons, if they so desire, to rejuvenate their inward powers. Much depends on what one does with one's leisure or, more precisely, by what one understands leisure to be. To some, it means just marking time—until the end. On that assumption, unoccupied time becomes a source of misery rather than happiness. But true leisure is a positive attitude of the mind and a renewing condition of the soul.[19]

Properly understood, leisure helps us see the world in a way that is different from ordinary experience. It gives us an opportunity to draw into ourselves the deeper realities of our existence. Leisure is a creative use of our time that, among other things, keeps tedium at bay. We should also understand how much it distances us from the demands of labor. Older persons are generally unemployed, but the habits of work can still influence what they do. For

---

19. Here I depend upon the classic study by Josef Pieper, *Leisure, The Basis of Culture* (South Bend, IN: St. Augustine's Press, 1998).The work was originally published in 1948. In *Learn To Grow Old*, Tournier affirms the value of leisure that is balanced by a recognition of the importance of work.

many, not to be obviously active is to be idle. They may admit the value of reflective or poetic thinking, but only if it is laborious, undertaken with great seriousness and energy. However, genuine leisure is compatible with rest and incompatible with simply "being busy." When we are passive but alert, our inner powers become more receptive. We can dwell lovingly upon all that is given to us in creation. To study at leisure is to experience delights rather than exhaustion.

For a satisfying old age, our minds must overcome that "dull incredulity" that can become habitual in the advancing years. While much feeling has been lost, our minds can still be turned toward interesting subjects. These can range over any area of thought, from a history of sports to the most subtle of metaphysical ideas. What matters is that we take up whatever suits our inclinations, experiences, and circumstances. As for motivation, a simple desire for greater understanding should suffice, yet some contend that in our advanced years we should be drawn only to reflection by our strongest passions. There is confusion here. The intellectual life is not driven by intense emotion. Furthermore, reflective thought is attracted to what is general and impersonal. Passing beyond what is concrete and immediate, leisurely contemplation yields a quiet pleasure—a higher enjoyment that comes from the broader aspects of our common human nature.[20]

Being involved in the world of knowing, of seeing what is true in itself, brings great enrichment and helps us to come more fully in touch with the substance of our personalities. Moreover, while originating in solitude, our thoughtfulness can also be of great social benefit. For one thing, it makes us more interesting, and to that degree, more attractive to the company of others. But it should also draw us toward a more inclusive range of community. One of the great challenges for older people is to fill out the public as well as the private aspects of their individual lives. Reflection

---

20. Compare Susan Jacoby, *Never Say Die: The Myth and Marketing of the New Old Age* (New York, NY: Pantheon Books, 2011), which seems to be driven by the assumption that passion is indispensable to all aspects of life, including that of reflective thought.

draws us to what is common about our shared human nature, and the understanding that none of us are entire unto ourselves. It follows that an interest in others and their good inheres in the power of thought.

In the past, a small leisure class made most of the important contributions to civilization. This minority was responsible for significant advances in science, politics, and culture. Now, in this more democratic age, the creative task is set in a broader framework. Those who develop the essentials of good living are, logically, drawn from the many; unfortunately, most are preoccupied with the worlds of commerce and the economy, as well as the demands of family life. Responsibility for the improvement of the broader community falls, in large measure, to older persons who are themselves a part of the expanding population; unlike the rest, however, they have time to address larger issues because they are not caught up in the demands of making a living. Emerson's dictum that seniors are those "who fear no cities and by whom cities stand," though stated long ago, has an important contemporary relevance.[21]

One of the characteristics of our political life is its divisiveness and ever more marked polaritites. To turn a metaphor, politics has become war by other means. These dispositions reflect the hermetic quality of the mass mentality. Modern populations, raised in an industrial and technological age, are inclined to direct their lives by seizing upon a limited aspect of the moral life and zealously defend their sense of the good with a fierce emotional attachment. Being so disposed, they close their minds to the more divergent and complex aspects of ethical or political life. They also close down the collaborative dimensions of co-existence that are indispensable to pluralistic democratic living. The problem was identified nearly a century ago by the British philosopher Bertrand Russell. He described the politics of his own time in a way that could well apply to our own:

---

21. Where life is true and noble, " . . . we have quite another sort of seniors than the frowzy, timorous, peevish dotards who are falsely old – namely, the men who fear no city, but by whom cities stand . . . ." Ralph Waldo Emerson, "Old Age," in *Society and Solitude*.

> [T]he world at present is full of angry self-centered groups, each incapable of viewing human life as a whole. Each willing to destroy civilization rather than yield an inch. To this narrowness no amount of technical instruction will provide an antidote.[22]

How should older persons react to this state of affairs? Should they treat these grave social and political disorders as simply a part of the pageant of life that they are condemned to watch from the sidelines? Or does this terrible situation provide an opportunity for them to give back to society what is its due? All men and women who are of advanced age should be alert to opportunities to make some return for all the resources that society provides to sustain them. For with wisdom born of experience, seniors can help a society that is extremely busy but, in its restlessness, is "racing to nowhere."

Today, many libraries throughout the country are hosting "Conversation Salons" or forums for collaborative discussions of important public issues. Their purpose is to provide a venue that is as free as possible from the one-sidedness of political ideologies and promote a civil exchange of ideas and opinions. Older men and women have much to contribute to these discussions. Their long experience has built up within them a unique capacity for understanding what is at stake in the most contentious public issues. Interpreting information through the lens of reflective thought, they transcend the limits of "data." Their emotions are more under control. Moreover, they have the ability to connect past and present with the future, even as most of society is stuck in the here and now. While open to change, seniors are better able than those younger than themselves to distinguish what is passing from what endures.

The public face of an older generation is the paramount repository of collective wisdom. Liberated from the struggle for power and prestige, those of advanced years are now free to tell the truth. Their role can even be prophetic. But they must choose to assume such positions if they are to regain any moral authority.

---

22. Bertrand Russell, *In Praise of Idleness and Other Essays at 48* (London: George Allen & Unwin, 1935).

Without such determination, seniors simply abandon what they have created and allow the direction of the world to fall into the hands of the selfish, but powerful, few.[23]

Composed of persons of different ages, Conversation Salons involve an exchange of ideas that has no generational boundaries. They provide an excellent chance for persons in different stages of life to better understand each other and learn how all can make valuable contributions to the common good. What is unique about the participation of seniors is that, being more detached from strong passions, they are able to make balanced and unhurried judgments about political problems. Moreover, they have a conciliatory capacity that can reconcile what seem to be intractable differences. They can serve as peacemakers as well as advocates of public understanding.

Unfortunately, many who have reached, or passed, the age of retirement find that having some form of employment is a financial necessity. Others of advanced age continue working because they enjoy doing so and because it gives them a continuing sense of being useful. But those economic realities should not obscure the fact that the most important service of the elderly is one of enlightenment, not labor. Even when older persons are out of touch with the vitalities of the workplace, they have much to contribute to the well being of the broader communities. For it is the wisdom that older persons have to offer that is of greatest value to the human enterprise. They make this available even when, ironically, they are disengaged from the ordinary world of the active life.

The wisdom of the elderly is especially needed for dialogue on any issue relating to violence. They understand best the destructive consequences of resorting to force whether in a domestic or a foreign policy context. Regarding the pressing issue of gun control, for example, ordinary men and women of advanced age can contribute much of the "common sense" that is needed to control the inflated rhetoric on rights that is too often used to block meaningful and serious reform. On other public issues of great importance, prior training and experience have a special value.

---

23. See Joan Chittister, op.cit.

The work of Alan Simpson has already shown how older persons have much to offer with respect to the issue of fiscal responsibility, and many others who have had careers in banking and investment can make comparable contributions. If properly motivated, they could provide wise counsel concerning the need for, as well as the limits of, regulations on investment.[24]

Most retired men and women have been freed from the struggles of making a living and thus better appreciate the value of work and economic activity with reference to other essential values. Unemployment is a terrible curse, especially for the young, and those of advanced years should do what they can to relieve it, even if such improvements would adversely affect their own interests and privileges. But such a response does not exhaust the question of what constitutes a full and happy life. In order to explore those larger questions, those living a long life must register their dissent from some of the major myths that direct the common life. They must especially challenge the premise that the endless consumption of goods and services must be the only objectives of a life well spent. The wisdom of the old can make a meaningful distinction between living to work and working to live. In public conversation they must place economics in perspective. They must have the courage to articulate the difference between life in its fullness and the destructive cult of endless labor fueled by the insatiable craving for material things.

Older persons should also protest the perversions of the major media, which subject social communication to the crass objectives of the market economy. It has been said that the enjoyment of music should not be interrupted by commercials, but apparently the visual fields of entertainment are not subject to such restraints. The general objective of those in control of electronic media seems to be stupefying audiences with trivial or vulgar programs, even as technological improvements have vastly increased the number of available channels. If some enjoyment or understanding is being derived from watching a particular show, a constant intrusion

---

24. See Alan Simpson and Erskine Bowles, *Report of the National Commission on Fiscal Responsibility and Reform,* Dec. 1, 2010.

of advertisements breaks up any development of thought in the mind of the viewer. To make matters worse, the whole business is sustained by the passive acceptance of a servile public. In our democracy, people will struggle vigorously for the expansion of personal liberty, yet the vast majority seem willing to accept the manipulation of their needs and wants through the commercialization of major media. The general public does not realize how much their choices as well as their sense of self-esteem are being taken from them by the advertising business. It is up to those now removed from the cycles of work and mindless entertainment to remind the rest of the population what their submission to these forces is doing to their inherent dignity, namely: impeding their personal growth and removing the country further and further away from the possibilities of a civilized existence.

This deeper understanding of temporal issues can be of great help to the succeeding generations. Older citizens can envision a world that is not only welcoming to all, but also raises all, including themselves, to higher levels of fulfillment. But if they are to be in the vanguard of genuine progress, the elders must themselves have a desire for personal as well as social improvement. They must realize that, if they are to promote the greater good of society at large, they must first change their own dispositions. While they may be reasonably content with the material conditions of their lives, older persons should not be satisfied with the moral condition of their souls. They should first reform themselves; in particular, they must avoid, or if necessary overcome, the vices that have throughout history been traditionally associated with old age. They need to confront their own narrow-mindedness and self-absorption as well as any willful isolation from the world around them. They must master the tendency to cling to the past while being contemptuous of the present. Most of all, those living a long life must conquer the disqualifying fear of the future. Otherwise, their opinions will be justly ignored.

By being open-minded and having a generous attitude, older persons can undertake that growth in virtue such as was recommended by Dante in his *Convivio*. There, it will be recalled, the great Christian humanist looked upon every stage of life, including that of old age, as a mixture of ascent and descent. As for the elderly, a development into higher virtues is possible even as they are in physical decline. If those living into the advanced years will morally and mentally mature, they can begin to attain a perfection that is to the advantage of others as well as themselves.

And yet there is more. While the quest for maturity in old age requires a renaissance of our mental and moral powers, it also calls us to the contemplation of beauty as much as it attracts us to the true and the good. Women have always understood this; many men still need to learn it. The beautiful is one of the essential properties of being, and aesthetic delight rises from all that which, upon being seen, or heard, pleases. The appreciation of whatever is lovely in nature, in crafts, painting, poetry, and indeed in all the fine arts, not only delights; it also draws us towards the divine. As Baudelaire put it, the instinct of beauty allows us to have a glimpse of heaven.[25]

Again, we transcend the demands of overt labor! This peaceful retirement into the depths of our being through the arts is a form of repose rather than idleness. The harmony, proportion, and radiance that we experience in all such pleasures come to us in a quietness that is refreshing to the soul. While our deepest energies are awakened, we are also freed from the anxieties that plague our daily existence. Here we come into contact with who we really are in a way not determined by others. Yet we have a strong desire to share with others the pleasures that have come to us through our senses. This desire to share whatever profoundly moves us is a mark of an expansive personality. Such generosity can, of course, exist at any age, but it has a special place in the lives of those living in advanced years. For here is that magnanimity that Dante identified as the highest virtue of the noble older person. Like a rose, the soul that has experienced the joys of the beautiful must open out and "give forth the fragrance generated within it."[26]

---

25. See, generally, Jacques Maritain, *Creative Intuition in Art and Poetry*, The A. W. Mellon lectures in the Fine Arts (New York: Meridian Books, 1955).

26. Dante, *Convivio*, Chapter XXVII.

Relationships

The effort towards finding our true selves is a lifetime project, but in old age it becomes more inner directed. There can be much self-pity as we pass into the later years, but there can also be a genuine growth through deliberate self-determination. Since this is a time of restraint as well as affirmation, the qualities of a virtuous life take on new meaning. Making prudent judgments about our lifestyle helps us to live in a balanced way and to manage artfully our physical and social limitations. Temperance is renewed through simplicity of diet. Furthermore, while becoming more aware of the conditions for a healthy body, we also become conscious of the need to promote a healthy mind. The loss of regular employment becomes a temptation to sloth unless we re-energize the powers of intellect and imagination that may have been largely dormant for many years.

The wisdom of the past assures us that in old age it is as important to attend to the needs of the mind as to those of the body. If we do so, reflection gradually takes precedence over action. But we must not allow our mental activity to become nothing more than self-conscious musings over our seemingly dismal circumstances. The antidote is to turn our minds outward and begin to contemplate the wonders that lie beyond us. As we have explained, leisure may lead us to an understanding of all that flows towards us from the created world. Through such an interaction between what is within and what is without, we experience a growth that builds up the deepest substance of our personalities.

Reflection arises in solitude, but it gradually draws us towards community. Any meditation upon the nature of the good eventually leads us to considerations of the common good. As with the Conversation Salons, we can be drawn into collaborative discussion of public issues. Leaving behind our more personal concerns, we move into the broadest relationships that constitute the makings of a civilized democracy. At the same time, at this level of discourse relationships are civil, but not necessarily intimate. A much greater part of the relatedness that makes up our advanced years is of an interpersonal nature. The quality and extent of these relationships have a great influence upon our prospects for longevity. How well or ill we live out these more particular encounters with others will largely determine how far we travel on the road to maturity.

The most fundamental relationships are those of marriage and family. In the previous chapter we noted the observations of the psychologist G. Stanley Hall concerning the value of spousal love in the later years, especially in the more spiritual qualities of this most intimate of relationships. The value of marriage prevails in spite of the increase of mutual responsibility and inevitable loss, and one who remains a devoted husband or wife until the final parting is an edifying example of personal maturity. Unfortunately, the relationships that older persons have with their offspring and descendants are much more problematic.

Age segregation is one of the most pervasive and unsettling aspects of modern life. It is especially damaging to self-esteem, because no one, at any stage of life, can establish personal worth in isolation from others. The difficulty is that, as we have come to honor the various stages of life as being important in themselves, we have accepted the fact that those who are living in these distinct phases tend to be closed in within themselves. All of us, from childhood on, share the interests and values of our own age group, and also care little for those who are at a different stage of life. Few are willing to reach beyond those of a similar age to seek that fuller humanism that would involve more communication across as well as within generations.

Part of the problem lies with cultural ideals. In the United States we tend to believe that all happiness is singular, and this emphasis upon solitary fulfillment poisons the wellspring of life in its most basic expression:

> . . . By insisting that each of us has more worth alone than we do collectively, by saying in the market place and in the home that people of different ages have nothing to say to one another, the family can have no value. But without the emotional net that the family can provide for its members, who may feel profoundly discouraged or

Reflections On Old Age

lonely, it is increasingly difficult for most people to enjoy a longer and healthier life with any grace.[27]

What has happened is that in the process of becoming a rich and progressive nation we have failed to grow socially, particularly in matters of family life. A mutual sharing becomes a curse rather than a blessing. Both young and old have set themselves apart from one another. And the most painful loss for the elderly is the loss of companionship with their descendants.

The relatedness that is so important to maturity may center in the family, but even where those relationships are happy and fulfilling, they should not become exclusive. At every stage of life human beings need to have associations outside of the home, and old age is no exception. Indeed, it is well established that there is a strong correlation between the warmth of all of our relationships and the health and happiness that we may experience in the final years of life.

Here some distinctions of gender become significant. Women are naturally drawn to the company of other women, and this is especially the case if they are widowed. They develop various forms of association that can help lift the burden of what might otherwise be an unendurable loneliness. Moreover, a cheerful attitude enriches the character as well as giving benefit to others. An older woman who takes a joy in living reflects her own self-sufficiency and gives the gift of hope to those she encounters.

Older men's relationships with each other are more problematic. Whether he is married or widowed, an older man is more cautious in his encounters with other men. This may perhaps have something to do with a residual feeling of rivalry that was part of his formative years, or it may be a natural aspect of the masculine drive towards personal independence. Whatever the cause, whenever older men encounter each other, it is not easy to break down the barriers of suspicion that obstruct the development of meaningful relationships. However, if the individual is open to

---

27. Victoria Secunda, *By Youth Possessed: The Denial of Age in America* (New York: Bobbs-Merrill Company, 1984), 155.

others, he will see the advantages of such real, though limited, companionships.

The gathering of men together has been, in one form or another, a constant of human history. During the middle years of life, when one is getting ahead in business or forging a professional career, associations of men are formed mainly for utilitarian purposes. One joins a group or club to promote one's own interests. For men in retirement, new forms of collective companionship arise simply from the shared experience of aging in proximity. Now getting together is more informal and more communal in nature. It may consist of just "talking shop" over coffee—a matter of sharing memories or opinions on contemporary issues. Differences must not become divisive. One thing that is held in common by the participants is an almost desperate need to talk—a need that expresses in a poignant way how deep is the loneliness of old age: thus the incessant searching by the elderly to find someone to listen to them and respond. Where the conversation is not especially personal, it is usually of little substance, but a spirit of playfulness laced with laughter often pleasantly makes up for what is lacking.

Some fear laughter, since it can be at another person's expense, yet there can be no doubt of its tonic quality. Mirth enlivens the spirit as much as it relieves the tensions of life. It is a wonderful remedy for the vice of self-centeredness. Even in advanced years men remain in some sense boys. Being able to enjoy a joke is part of the initiation. A new member of a group of older men may find himself being tested not on his abilities or status, but rather, and more importantly, on his sense of humor. These experiences develop a sense of comradeship and belonging that is emotionally beneficial. Through such gatherings men come to be familiar with each other and develop bonds of respect and affection. And yet there is something incomplete about such experiences. Our human nature naturally moves us in the direction of deeper attachments and understandings.

Friendship in the classical sense is not thought of favorably in the modern world. This is in part a consequence of the accelerated pace of our lives that disperses the attention needed to cultivate a close relationship and perhaps also because of misplaced fears of homosexuality. Yet even in old age both men and women need the company of someone like themselves who happens to have similar interests and values. Over time, there develops a mutual reliance in matters of need. What two or more men or women share deeply in common may bring mutual delight, but it can also set them apart from the remainder of the larger group to which they also belong. Those with whom there is no intimacy may resent the exclusion. This is a traditional problem. Communities of older men or older women can feel as threatened by special friendships as any other social group. Yet having a friend in this fuller sense is one of the precious elements of human happiness, and it should not be sacrificed to any superficial uniformity of tastes or interests.[28]

There is a further complication. When one lives in any community comprised essentially of the elderly, more immediate responsibilities limit the time available for the development of particular friendships. In such communities there are many in various degrees of suffering and neediness, not only because of obvious infirmities but also because of the deep loneliness and sense of isolation that may overshadow old age. Daily one meets someone who needs some attention, even if it is only in patiently listening or offering a kind word. In these situations there is an obligation to be not just cheerful but also friendly—even when there is otherwise no deep sharing of mutual interests. One must try to understand more than be understood. Compassion also requires that, as far as possible, we make the other's situation our own. In this way a fellowship that is deeper and wider than natural friendship begins to define the character of these more extensive relationships.

When reaching out in friendship, or in mercy, to another older person, the intention is to affirm the other in his or her uniqueness while, at the same time, preserving one's own distinctive

---

28. For a basic defense of friendship, see C. S. Lewis, *The Four Loves* (Glasgow, Scotland: William Collins and Sons, 1960), Ch. 4. See also the study of former President Jimmy Carter, *The Virtues of Aging*, Ch. 15 (New York: Ballantine Publishing – Library of Contemporary Thought, 1998). Carter also strongly supports the value for older people of volunteering. *The Virtues of Aging*, Ch. 12.

identity. Such encounters are indefinite, but as such they bring to completion only the horizontal dimensions of human relatedness. Since the vertical aspect of our being remains, some basic choices must be faced. If we are foolish, we will limit our connective expectations to the horizons of this world; if wise, in these final years we will come to understand that it is only in relationship with God that we can become fully human.

In old age, as in every other phase of existence, there is a desire for deep and lasting happiness. Experience shows us that this essential aspiration is always in tension with the forces of evil as well as those that inhere in the imperfections of life on earth. As we advance into our later years, the balance seems to tip more toward disappointment and frustration. Mortality intrudes into our experience more persistently, especially as an increasing number of friends and relatives pass away. In these conditions we can be overcome by sorrow and made even sadder by a sense of remorse for our past mistakes. We reach a point of helplessness and need for forgiveness that no human agency, however well intentioned, can supply. More positively, we have also received the gift of longevity. There are many human causes for extended life, but essentially it is a gift of Divine Providence. We also need to express a gratitude for the gift, directing such thankfulness to the One from whom all blessings flow.[29]

We have the assurance of St. Paul that, even as we outwardly decline, we can be inwardly renewed. And it is by means of prayer as well as the sacramental life that we sustain a relationship with God and, in so doing, recover the joy of our youth. In the Christian economy, we are called to pray for others as well as for ourselves. Beginning with our parents and siblings, we pray for all who have

---

29. "At every stage of life it is necessary to be able to discover the presence and blessing of the Lord and the riches they bring. We must never let ourselves be imprisoned by sorrow! We have received the gift of longevity. Living is beautiful even at our age. In our faces may there always be the joy of feeling loved by God and not sadness." Pope Benedict XVI, "Reflections on Frustration and Joys of Aging," *Address to the Elderly in Care* at Rome, Feb. 12, 2013, in *The Tablet*, 16 Feb. 2013. See also *Letter of Pope John Paul II to the Elderly* (1999).

been dear to us over the long term of our lives, and do so without regard to whether or not they are still amongst us. We pray for those both near and far and for those whom we have injured, as well as for those who have done us harm. Praying with faith and constancy strengthens the bonds of our intimate as well as remote relationships. It also elevates our understanding of the value of a long life, encouraging us to enjoy all its possibilities and to see longevity as the last stage of our extended journey into human maturity.[30]

---

30. "No wonder we do not lose heart! Though our outward humanity is in decay, yet day by day we are inwardly renewed . . . ," St. Paul, 2 Cor 4: 8-17.

4

Last Things

The Fear of Death

IN 2006, PHILIP ROTH, one of America's most distinguished and prolific writers, published a novella titled *Everyman*. It is the story of a thrice-married unnamed commercial artist in his seventies, who has moved from New York City to a retirement village near the sea in New Jersey. Each year his health problems multiply, and he must endure numerous hospitalizations for procedures related to his heart. With the exception of his daughter, he is completely alone, haunted in the bleakness of his existence by the sense that he is nearing the end of his days. He is increasingly aware that "the great calamity death is waiting in the wings."[1]

Before he reached old age, an insatiable lust had made the protagonist a serial adulterer, which had ruined his marriages. Sexual pleasure, now virtually lost, had been his deepest delight. When sexually alive, he was, he thought, fully human. But sexuality had a deeper meaning. It also pointed to the foundations of his existence. He had become convinced that his being was fundamentally carnal, that his body was his ultimate reality, and that it lived, and would die, according to terms set by the bodies of all who had preceded him.

In his old age, the idea of spiritual immortality has no place in his assessment of the nature of his existence. Nor do the consolations of religion. He had decided long ago that all religions were fraudulent and, even worse, unworthy of an adult life. For him, as

---

1. Philip Roth, *Everyman* (New York: Houghton Mifflin, 2006) 41.

extinction approaches, there will be no childish talk of death and God or fantasies about a final celestial home.

His only consolation lies in his memories of childhood. He revives his recollections of the happiness of his adolescent years as well as the joy of being a child in a secure home and family. As with Proust, the perfect is something behind, not ahead. There is an implicit rejection of the Abrahamic tradition in which the one who lives with faith sets forth on a journey towards an unknown country that God will finally reveal to him.

Everyman is an extreme imaginative expression of secular destiny. But it reflects a widely held view in modern Western culture about the temporal limits of any expectations of human happiness. In summary, as has been well stated by Julian Barnes:

> We encourage one another toward the modern secular Heaven of self-fulfillment: The development of the personality, the relationships that help define us, the status-giving job, the material goods, the ownership of property, the foreign holidays, the acquisition of savings, the accumulation of sexual exploits, the visits to the gym, the consumption of culture. It all adds up to happiness, doesn't it—doesn't it?[2]

The idea of secular fulfillment as a final goal of human life has many advocates, especially among those who have the controlling power or considerable influence in education, media, and politics. But to an agnostic temperament, this modern humanism can be as delusional a myth as the Christianity that it has sought to displace. Even if the Christian view was false, it remained attractive to the imagination as a form of "supreme fiction," whereas the secular conception, especially when supported by Darwinian principles, remains, to the thoughtful mind, something from which one should withhold complete assent.[3]

---

2. Julian Barnes, *Nothing To Be Afraid Of* (New York: Alfred Knopf, 2008), 59.

3. Barnes, op. cit. According to Joseph Ratzinger (Pope Emeritus Benedict XVI), the modern world is caught in a double dissatisfaction – with religion, but also with scientific explanations of the most important humanistic

The idea that the world of our experience is completely self-sufficient has ardent supporters, but it does not satisfy the desire for a greater understanding of the meaning and purpose of human life. Modern man is dissatisfied with both the religious and the scientific explanations of existence, and these complex feelings are exacerbated by the fear of death. *Everyman* is literally true, at least for the majority of those who, having reached old age, are especially sensitive to the terminal nature of their existence. But dread is not the only description of their feelings. It is also true that older persons can teach us how to die as well as how to live—to learn to love life without being paralyzed by a constant fear of death. It is among the elderly that the Abrahamic ideal makes the greatest sense, because, as we age, we more deeply understand that in the propensities of our lives we have always been on the way toward some unknown future. In old age, the nature of that future, and the way it is to be anticipated, become issues of paramount importance.[4]

To the men of the Enlightenment, the traditional Christian understanding that temporal existence is just a trial or preparation for what follows after death was offensive. The progressive minds thought that such a conception of human purpose threatened the developing awareness of the importance of life on earth. To a thinker such as Montaigne, all religion was based upon contempt for life. He would counter with contempt for death—a contempt that he believed would give us a pleasant taste for living. Rather than indulging in the fear of dying, he thought that we should have it constantly in mind, facing it head-on with awareness and attention. It is interesting to compare Montaigne's approach with that of Cicero. In *De Senectute* the great Roman recognized that, when

issues. *Faith and the Future* (San Francisco: Ignatius Press, 2009).

4. Recent sources of wisdom about Old Age include Joan D. Chittister, *The Gift of Years: Growing Old Gracefully* (New York: Blue Ridge, 2008); Simone de Beauvoir, *The Coming of Age* (New York: G. D. Putnam, 1972); John LaFarge, S. J., *Reflections on Growing Old* ((New York: The America Press, 1963); Sherwin B. Nuland, *The Art of Aging* (New York: Random House, 2007); Paul Tournier, *Learn to Grow Old* (Louisville, KY: Westminster/John Knox Press, 1972). The Abrahamic Ideal and its relation to Christianity is explained by Pope Francis in his Encyclical Letter, *The Light of Faith,* Chapter One (2013).

we reach old age, we cannot be far from death, and he was well aware of how this can cause us greater torment than anything in earlier stages of life. But for Cicero, the worrying was unnecessary. There are only two possible consequences of dying: either total extinction, or the passage of our souls to some place where we shall live forever. While much of modern reflection is obsessed with the prospect of extinction, for Cicero, that possibility was of little importance. Final happiness was what was desirable, and he was certain that an eternal life lay ahead for him that would involve a reunion with those whom he had loved and admired. Although he did, in fact, die by violence, Cicero believed that, for the old, death usually came more peacefully than it does for the young. Dying in old age means death in the fullness of time—like coming into a harbor after a long journey. Unlike Montaigne, Cicero also thought that, from our earliest years, we should discipline ourselves to make light of death and, further, that the man who does not so train himself can never experience peace of mind.[5]

Cicero's philosophy of death and dying reflects the Platonists' view that, upon our demise, our soul is released from its imprisonment in the body. Cicero was covering all the bases by recognizing the possibility of extinction even though he did not favor that option. But those who did believe that, at the end, there was nothing could find some solace in the philosophy of Epicurus. If death meant extinction, it was important that during life we enjoy—in a moderate way—the sensual pleasures available to the living body. Careful readers will catch some link between the Epicurean way, with its affirmation of physical life, and the sensuality of the character developed by Philip Roth in *Everyman,* although there the bodily pleasures are more limited and intense than in traditional Epicureanism. Nevertheless, the novel provides a contemporary example of the carnal logic that follows a rejection of the spiritual side of human nature. On the other hand, the pagan outlook expressed in Cicero's treatise will bear some limited and qualified

---

5. Michel de Montaigne, *Essais* (New York: The Heritage Press, 1946), 20. See also the discussion in Barnes, op.cit., 60. Cicero's views on death are found in *De Senectute,* Chapters VII and VIII.

comparison with what came to be the Christian perspective on death and eternal life.[6]

Consider Dante. Recall how this great humanist believed that a person who has reached old age does not simply enjoy the acclaim that follows his previous accomplishments. Rather, as he ages, he can still grow in moral virtue as well as in charity. This was part of Dante's view of nobility, by which he did not mean a distinction of social class, but rather the overall perfection of human nature—a fulfillment that for him surpasses any form of happiness that may otherwise be found on earth.

In the final years, according to Dante, the noble soul prepares for a return to God. He describes this process as heading for " . . . the port whence she set out when she first entered upon the sea of this life." The soul blesses the voyage she has made, as this journey has been one of goodness and magnanimous virtue. In this Christian perspective, natural death is not a time of storm and bitterness, but rather the coming to a serene haven and repose in gentleness and peace.[7]

This ideal conception of the end of human life was not favored by others in Dante's time. For one thing, there was no general class of the elderly as such. Furthermore, the Church was itself drawing a grim portrait of the future prospects of all who die, an approach that did much to encourage a fear of death. Other broad developments, such as the Renaissance and the Reformation, further weakened the links between time and eternity.

The joy of Redemption was gradually slipping into eclipse. The contrast between medieval asceticism and the evolving religious atmosphere was a striking example of the changes. While severely penitential, medieval practices had celebrated the brightness of heaven and distinguished it from the darkness of this world. Puritanism, by contrast, although it attributed religious significance

---

6. The popular image of Epicureanism is that it encourages unrestrained physical pleasure, but the original philosophy was more austere. See Epicurus, *The Art of Happiness* (New York: Penguin Books, 2012).

7. Dante, *The Banquet*, Book IV. There is a fuller discussion of Dante's view of old age in Chapter One of the present work.

to temporal vocations, thought of the eternal as stormy and unapproachable. Liturgically, the earlier mentality wanted the church service to be expressive and the vestments of the priest to be colorful. The Puritan insisted upon a stark and somber ceremony, with the preachers clad in gowns of black.

As time went on, a stress upon severity and a generally somber tone began to spread throughout all of Christianity. Little was done to encourage believers of any denomination to cultivate hope in an eternal happiness. Then, with the advance of science and technology, expectations of immortality were virtually extinguished. The human soul was beginning to be thought of as one of the features of the brain rather than a distinct entity with transcendent yearnings.[8]

The decline of faith in a life after death was felt in America as well as in Europe. Here the problem was exacerbated by the strong influence of New England Calvinism. Images of human beings as "sinners in the hands of an angry God," along with doctrines of predestination, were promoted by the great theologian Jonathan Edwards and became widely influential. Every effort was made to keep the sinful multitudes in the fear of God and resigned to the probable prospect of damnation. These traditions were gradually challenged by more humanistic ideas that stressed the importance of a positive understanding of personal identity and destiny. The struggle between these opposing views would eventually turn speculation towards the decisive issues of personal immortality.[9]

Early in the twentieth century, Elizabeth Gardner Jordon, the then editor of *Harper's Bazaar*, invited contributions to a symposium on the future life, from writers and celebrities of her time as well as from some less eminent literary figures. Among the best known were William Dean Howells, Henry James, and Julia Ward Howe. Their contributions were published in the magazine between April

---

8. There is a good discussion of these changes in G. K. Chesterton, *Chaucer* (New York: Sheed & Ward, 1956).

9. I explore these developments in my study, *Person and Society in American Thought* (New York: Peter Lang, 2007), Chapter One.

1909 and February 1910. In that same year, the reflections were published in a book titled *In After Days: Thoughts on the Future Life.*

In an introductory essay, Howells concentrated his attention upon the importance of grief, expressed as sorrow over the loss of a loved one. He distinguished these sentiments from brooding over death; that is, genuine sorrow is a lament that can even be cheerful and willing to help the affliction of others. The fact of death does not raise the issue of personal immortality as strongly as it affects the deepest aspiration of our souls for recovery of a companionship that has been lost by the dying of one's loved ones. For consolation, Howells recommends traditional religious sources, while recognizing that neither divine nor apostolic assurances any longer provide the hope that they once did. Now the pain of loss can be assuaged by the insights of poets, as well as by dreams and visions. And he reminds his readers that time heals all wounds, even those caused by death. While he cannot share the absolute faith of some, Howells waits patiently for the fulfillment of hopes that Christianity has drawn more from Greek philosophy (such as Socrates' attitude towards death) than from the biblical prophets. Now being himself old, he finds consolation in a saying of his father's: "Youth is the time to believe; age is the time to trust." That fits in well with his agnosticism, as he observes, "There are many things that I doubt, but few that I deny; where I cannot believe, there I often trust."[10]

Howells's reflections were followed by those of Elizabeth Stuart Phelps, a well-known writer of the time, who had published fifty-seven volumes of fiction, poetry, and essays. She wrote one widely popular book, *The Gates Ajar* (1868), to comfort women who had lost loved ones during the Civil War. In this work and in other writings she had challenged the gloomy Calvinist version of heaven. Her contribution to *In After Days* was titled "The Great Hope."

---

10. William Dean Howells, "A Counsel of Consolation," in *In After Days*, 3-16. Howell believed that sorrow does not exclude cheerfulness, especially in trying to be helpful to those who have lost a loved one.

Like Howells, Phelps concentrated on the phenomenon of bereavement. She saw its consequences as catastrophic, filled with fear and unreason, unless the one who grieves is led to an acceptance by God. Memory connected with death was also a torment for the grieving party, who could not help recalling how he or she had injured the one now deceased. Yet remorse has consolation in the thought that love forgives and that we can place no limits upon the powers of the dead to remit the injuries.

What is virtually unbearable is the "apparent" finality of death. Everlasting farewells pierce the depths of human despair. But these pains cannot be relieved by unbelief. Phelps was contemptuous of those who denied the possibility of human immortality. Whatever may be the force of the arguments for extinction upon death, they are not subtle enough to satisfy human feeling. Love is greater than reason, and it is in the affections where the convincing arguments for immortality can be found. But the primary issue for Phelps was that of persuading herself, and her audience, that God—who controlled both life and death—was a loving being.

The question of the Afterlife was of the greatest importance, because it implicated the very nature of God. To the Calvinists, His Sovereign Majesty was expressed in arbitrary power and vindictive justice. One of the founders of Unitarianism, William Ellery Channing, had effectively challenged this theology. Channing argued that if cruelty was a deficiency in a human being, it could hardly be an attribute of Divine Power and Beauty. The doctrine of Predestination was also untenable. That teaching had held that, with the exception of the Elect, the human race, as it passes through time, lives out the consequences of total corruption, and then, upon death, suffers eternal damnation. In this limited concept of Atonement, Christ had died just for those who were predestined for heaven—not for those whose ultimate destination was Hell.[11]

Phelps's reflections on these questions were interesting. She thought that the issue of personal immortality was bound up with

---

11. See William Ellery Channing, "The Moral Argument against Calvinism" (1809), in *The Works of William Ellery Channing D. D.* (Boston: The American Unitarian Association, 1875), 459-68.

our experience of life on earth. There had been many public as well as private tragedies in her lifetime, and she concluded that the sum was more of misery than of happiness. Life was truly "a vale of tears." If God was really good and not malevolent, He would be kind, and in that kindness provide some reimbursement for all the suffering that human beings endure while living out their lives. We should not believe that He would gratuitously be the dispenser of agony. Without some recompense after death in terms of personal immortality, life in this unhappy world would be little more than an "experiment in vivisection."[12]

For Phelps, Love is the greatest attribute of personality, and it is love alone that is capable of resolving the question of immortality. If God is a person, we must think of Him as loving rather than as vindictive. Her belief was that human love can approach that of the divine. When we love fully, we can anticipate an ultimate reunion with those who, once dear to us, have departed.

The composer of "The Battle Hymn of The Republic," Julia Ward Howe, offered her reflections to the Symposium under the title "Beyond the Veil." She recalled the great changes that had come during her lifetime: from her childhood, when images of the blessedness of heaven and the torments of hell were constantly offered to her youthful imagination, to the new century, where those ultimate images were generally fading from consciousness. Now, in her late maturity, she finds herself adrift upon a "boundless sea of conjecture," still seeking the ultimate harbor. Theodore Parker, a Unitarian preacher who insisted in maintaining a distinction between what was transient and what was permanent in Christianity, had been a helpful influence, leading her to conclude that some truths of lasting value had remained with her throughout her long life. The words of Christ filled our consciousness with thoughts of eternal things that would never change, no matter what happened in the evolution of the universe. Above all, He taught the eternal

---

12. "One may say with reverence . . . that the character of God itself is on trial in the history of this unfortunate world. Life is scarcely more than an experiment in vivisection if death is the end of personality." *In After Days*, 31.

hope that lies in God's eternal goodness: "What is best for you and me will be."[13]

Another important contribution came from the pen of Henry Mills Alden, an editor at *Harper's* who was also an eighth-generation descendant of the famous John Alden who came to America on the Mayflower. In 1895 Alden had published *A Study of Death*, which a review in *The New York Times* described as the most profound essay on mysticism ever published by an American. In his contribution to *In After Days*, Alden undertook to study "The Other Side of Mortality."

Alden begins by meditating on the importance of mortality to the progress of the human race. He looks upon the world as a continuous creation that calls for a broad and impersonal thanatopsis, or view of death. If life on earth were one of indefinite existence, it would be sterile and unproductive. The freshness of the race is assured only by successive generation. Mortality and the renewal of nativity provide the incentives to growth. Yet the greatest importance of the cycle of birth and dying is what it means to us in our personal experience.[14]

Like the medieval Christians, Alden is struck by the constant contrast between darkness and light. The deepest meaning of death cannot be expressed by dark dress or vestments, for blackness is the color of despair. For us to endure our coming and going,

---

13. *In After Days*, 89-103. Theodore Parker, who had a considerable influence on Julia Ward Howe, was an extraordinary Unitarian minister who worked in and around Boston in the early part of the nineteenth century. Having abandoned reliance upon Scripture, he tried to develop an evolutionary theism. See Henry Steele Commager, *Theodore Parker* (Boston: The Beacon Press, 1947).

14. H. M. Alden, "The Other Side of Mortality," in *In After Days*, 107-32. Alden adopted an evolutionary understanding of creation, seeing within that framework the positive value of death to human development on earth. Each new generation brought renewal and an increase in civilization. Some contemporary philosophers have argued that the decrease or extinction of future generations would adversely affect the living, since what they have valued will not be sustained after their deaths. See the review by Thomas Nagel, "After You're Gone," in *The New York Review of Books*, Vol.LXI, No.1, 26-28 (January 9, 2014).

the angel of death must become the angel of life. To Alden's mind, at the time of dying there must be a new horizon, a brightness that expands faith, hope, and love. While death closes one door, it opens another. Otherwise, we are defrauded by our mortality.

Since the time of Cicero, those who have speculated about a future life have thought of it in terms of reunion with loved ones who predeceased us. But for Alden, what was of primary importance was that upon death there be a continuation and fuller development of the individual personality. That was especially important to those who had accomplished much in their lifetimes. Given the importance of the unique personal life, he refused to think of immortality in terms of absorption of the individual into some Absolute. The goal was not the Nirvana of Buddhism, where perfect blessedness demanded the extinction of individual existence, but something that could be reconciled with what we know of ourselves and our character. Yet Alden concedes that the completion of the personal portrait brings us to the limits of imaginative understanding of the afterlife. In the end, mortality will cease, but what else a new life might involve exceeds our powers of comprehension.

A novel contribution to the essays was one by an Italian historian and man of letters, Guglielmo Ferrero. Ferrero was well known at the time. He had published a magisterial five-volume work on the history of Rome, been a guest of President Theodore Roosevelt, and also lectured in the northeastern parts of the United States. He had profound sociological insight into the reasons why the subject of life after death was not of interest to the general public.

Ferrero's study of the past, and his understanding of the present, led him to discover deep connections between otherwise very different civilizations. Now, among the democracies, as it was with the elites of ancient Rome, there was intemperance of personal ambition that was bound to bring disappointment:

> Riches, power, knowledge, do not increase our happiness, . . . for we also, like the Romans of the period of Augustus, place the end of living too much within ourselves. We lose faith in those ideals and beliefs that

propose to man an aim outside himself, beyond his own personal interests and pleasures and the time in which he lives.

Man cannot be happy unless he ardently longs for and awaits with assurance—which is more difficult than the longing—something he will not be able to obtain while he lives . . . unless he projects beyond the span of his own life a vital part of his aspirations and invests them with his living spiritual forces. If all his desires be fully circumscribed by the time in which he lives, what happens to a man?[15]

Whatever this beyond may be, it is within the reach of all, but any who wish to reach it must hope for something beyond their own time and the concerns of their own selves.

The final essay of *In After Days*, written by Henry James, bore the inquisitive title, "Is There Life after Death?" James believed that, the longer we live, the more intensely interesting the question becomes. Each must decide if he should either resign himself to the inevitable or reach out in some way to the transition at the end of earthly existence. James chose the latter path. But for him, his desire was not the one of traditional Scripture, where the soul longs for the coming of the Lord. The soul, which James equated with personality, was expressed in consciousness, and it was that which he hoped to extend, even though he knew that, like all mortals, he must die. He thought it would be unreasonable if immortality required a complete dissociation from the persons that we now know ourselves to be.

James's interest was in the artistic consciousness. This enriched his experience, as in his literary creativity he was able to comprehend, in imagination, the great variety of the world and its

---

15. Guglielmo Ferrero, "The Life after This," in *In After Days,* 188. Ferrero observed that modern man is rightly proud of his many accomplishments, but he is called upon to learn and to do too many things. There are negative consequences, because the too active life "spurns the contemplative, atrophies the imagination, habituates the spirit to heeding only concrete things." See *In After Days*, 186.

endless interrelations. His work as a writer brought him into communication with the fundamental sources of his existence:

> The very provocation offered to the artist by the universe, the provocation to him to be—poor man who may know so little of what he is in for!—an artist, and thereby supremely serve it; what do I take that for but the intense desire of being to get itself personally shared, to show itself ... personably sharable, and thus foster the sublimist faith?[16]

The enjoyment experienced by the artist in his maturity increases within him the desire for a renewal of existence. If, at death, it all came to nothing, the result would be a "practical joke of the lowest description." The artistic consciousness plays in the fountain of being, establishing relations of the highest nature. For James, this is all the great adventure of his personality; that being so, it is surely unlikely that at the time of death all connection with this development of the inner self should be lost.

For James, his understanding of ultimates does not constitute a religious faith in the orthodox sense. He has been led by inner desire to encourage the growth of an aesthetic consciousness; he could do nothing better to preserve his personal existence even if he believed. Through the development of that consciousness, he is persuaded that he is doing something to advance his own prospects of immortality.

Final Accounts

The various essays in the 1910 Symposium reveal the degree to which the oppressive Puritan theology that was developed in the early history of the United States was being overtaken by more hopeful views of human destiny. The Divinity was now being

---

16. "Is There Life after Death?" in *In After Days*, 224-25. For a general assessment of this essay, see Christopher Stuart, "Is There Life after Death? Henry James' Response to the New York Edition," in *The Colby Quarterly* 35.2 (1999) 90-101. The general view is that James did not believe in a future life, but rather that art provided whatever we can know about immortality.

thought of more as merciful than vindictive, and the fearful apprehension of death went into decline. There were rising expectations for reunion in some form of afterlife with those who predeceased us but with whom we were still bound in ties of affection. Of greatest importance was the emerging confidence in the preservation and extension of the individual personality into eternity. But with a single exception, in these essays there is no waiting with assurance for the Resurrection. Fragmentary references are made to the teachings of Christ that undoubtedly bring some consolation to the writers and their audiences, but they serve more as projections of subjective desires for happiness than as expressions of convictions that possess a sharable objectivity.[17]

It has been said that, in the modern world, the most fundamental division is no longer between those who believe and those who do not, but rather between those who fear death and those who can calmly face its coming. The formula is too simplistic, because the problem of dying, along with its consequences, is much more complex. Moreover, the subject is intellectually intriguing. The mind that is awake desires a more complete understanding of death and whatever may lie beyond our limited and painful life on earth. The simple assumption of extinction, or "total emptiness forever," may be poetically attractive, but it cannot replace the cumulative experience of the human race. The anticipation of some form of life beyond the grave is too deeply a part of human history to be imaginatively dismissed. Moreover, if the nature of the afterlife is the most compelling of human questions, it is important that it be approached with adequate resources of mind and heart. The challenges raised by the coming of death require access to the more extensive resources of faith as well as those of reason. Clearly, a mature thought and belief system desires to comprehend not only the contours of this life, but also whatever can be known of a

---

17. There is a more explicit discussion of the Christian view of death and resurrection in William Hanna Thomson, M. D., "The Future State," in *In After Days*, 155-75.

life to come. The one who is truly wise will try to understand, as far as possible, the relations between these two spheres of being.[18]

The essays that made up the 1910 book *In After Days* provide some incentives for reflective development. Perhaps the most important essay in the Symposium was that of Henry James. A distinguished novelist, he was the most prominent man of letters of his time. To him, the center of personal existence was self-consciousness, which he thought of as the core of the individual personality and as the repository of his artistic modes of being. He believed that the unlimited expansion of this consciousness would bring him into relationship with the ultimate sources of existence, where he could revel in an abundance of being. His conception bears some comparison with that of his brother, the philosopher William James, who argued that inwardly we can come to understand that our unique being is engaged with a wider, unseen universe.[19]

Self-consciousness has various aspects. For Henry James, the artistic was decisive, since he thought that it reflected his long labors in the field of literature. Moreover, these aesthetic endeavors had made him the person he thought that he had become in time and which he hoped to extend into eternity. However, if such a conception of being human is taken as a premise, it also seems logical to assume that the whole personal quality of our existence, as developed on earth, should pass into an afterlife, especially those aspects that record the quality of our moral behavior, because it is within the conscience of each person that the dramatic struggle between good and evil occurs. From ancient times, in both biblical and classical traditions, accountability at death of how we have

---

18. See the Introductory Statement of *The Pastoral Constitution on the Church in the Modern World* of the Second Vatican Council, where it is noted that it is the responsibility of the Church to respond to "the perennial questions which men ask about this present life and the life to come, and about the relationship of the one to the other."

19. It was the belief of William James that, in the depths of one's own being, the self can make contact with a wider self that is distinct from, but not discontinuous with, the unique individual. This mystical communion is the source of the particular person's active life. See *The Will to Believe and Other Essays in Popular Philosophy* (1909).

lived our lives—in either righteousness or wrongdoing—is what determines our final personal destiny.

Plato recommended that the elderly remember their moral behavior and show remorse for the evil they had done during the course of their lives, since they were soon to enter into a place of reward or punishment. Throughout the centuries, those who have written about old age have also expressed awareness that the nearness of death entails the proximity of judgment. In the Christian tradition, judgment awaits all who have reached the age of reason—a judgment both at the time of death and at the Second Coming of Christ. In addition to the alternatives of Heaven and Hell, the tradition also provides for a Purgatory, or a period of purification which, however painful, will be entirely different from the punishment of the dammed. The most graphic descriptions of the final end appear in the late scripture, *The Book of Revelation*, which provides the dramatic experience where the dead are judged on the record of their deeds, and all those whose names are not found in the roll of the living are cast down, with death and Hades, into the lake of fire.[20]

Powerful images of the Last Judgment, such as those that appeared in the artistic creations of medieval Europe, once caused great anxiety among believers; the fearfulness continued into the beginnings of the modern world. Such distress has largely disappeared in this post-conciliar age, as conceptions of Divine Vengeance have been replaced by increasing belief in Divine Love and Mercy. Yet both particular judgment and final judgment remain as integral parts of the teachings of the Church, and anyone approaching the end of life cannot afford to ignore them. However, it is of equal importance to understand the reasons for the continued relevance of these dogmas.

Among some Catholics and others of Protestant persuasion, an extraordinary confidence in Divine Grace can lead to an

---

20. Plato, *The Republic*, Part Eleven. The fiery images come from chapter on The Book of Revelation to John 20. See also *The Catechism of the Catholic Church*, Part One, Chapter Three, and John E. Thiel, *Icons of Hope: The Last Things in Catholic Imagination* (Notre Dame, IN: University of Notre Dame Press, 2013).

unwarranted assumption of personal righteousness as well as a hasty and discriminatory opinion about the number of those who will be forever saved or lost. Those with strong confidence in the certainty of their salvation have no doubts about their final destiny and they can easily become complacent about the availability of Divine Mercy. They can underestimate the power of evil both within themselves and in the world around them. However, true belief requires that we accept the opaque quality of the end time. We also need to be reminded that we are precluded from assuming that God's final Judgment is a foregone conclusion, either for us as individuals or for any other human being.[21]

Catholic tradition and teaching hold firmly to the belief that grace does not eclipse human responsibility. Grace perfects freely willed virtuous actions, however limited their range, while also giving special affirmation to acts of charity. Moral dereliction and uncharitable dealings with others will lead to appropriate punishment. This assessment of our doings must be carefully distinguished from Kantian principles, which express the conviction that after death we can legitimately expect a final happiness with God if our temporal actions were constituted of moral imperatives derived, a priori, by practical reason. For Kant, morality, being autonomous, is, in effect, its own reward. For the Christian, by contrast, cooperation with grace is indispensable to the attribution of eternal significance to the ways we conduct ourselves on earth. This intersection of grace and freedom serves not only in the working out of individual salvation but also in the building up of the communion of saints.[22]

It is evident from the essays reviewed concerning life after death that they proceed on the assumptions that the goal is one of personal immortality and that this everlastingness is spiritual, not carnal, in nature. Such assumptions extend into the modern age beliefs that were first developed in ancient cultures concerning the irrelevance of the corruptible body to any future bliss. In his essay

---

21. Thiel, op. cit.

22. Immanuel Kant, *Critique of Pure Reason*, trans. by N. K. Smith (New York: St. Martin's Press, 1965). See also Thiel, *Icons of Hope*, 3-6.

On Old Age, for example, Cicero followed the Platonic tradition concerning the absolute primacy of the soul. The theory was that, during our earthly sojourn, the soul is imprisoned in the body, while, at death, it ascends to its true celestial home. For Christians, however, belief in personal immortality equates to belief in a resurrection that is an extension to human beings of the Resurrection of Jesus Christ from the dead. In conformity to the experience of the Savior, there will be, at the Last Judgment, a rising of the whole human person, body and soul, as well as a final accounting of the course of human history.[23]

It is an inherent part of the Christian Credo that Jesus Christ will come again to judge the living and the dead. Contemplation of this Second Coming provides believers with an anticipatory image by which to measure the progress, or decline, of their love for God and for their neighbor. In daily life where, even into old age, the interior struggle between good and evil is continually enacted, the idea of the Last Judgment provides a provocation of one's conscience—a stimulus that runs much deeper than any ruminations in self-consciousness. It also raises an expectation of God's justice.

The dogma concerning a final judgment has lost much of its influence upon the lives of those who are otherwise believers. Part of the reason we have already noticed, namely: the extraordinary emphasis upon Divine Mercy that has developed among all Christian denominations. An individualistic sense of salvation is also an impediment to comprehensive understanding, since such a disposition is not open to a finality that encompasses the whole of the human race and its history. As for the evils that mar such total history, a confident ideal of progress takes it for granted that civilization can correct all injustice or, more modestly, that we should not leave all injustice to a future judge.[24]

---

23. *Catechism of the Catholic Church*, 997-1000; *Icons of Hope*, 17-23. See also Sacred Congregation for the Doctrine of the Faith, "Letter Concerning Certain Questions of Eschatology" (1979).

24. Pope John Paul II recognized the decline of sensitivity to Last Things among modern men and women, but he insisted that " . . . *faith in God as Supreme Justice* has not become irrelevant to man, the expectation remains that there is Someone who, in the end, will be able to speak the truth about the

There can be no doubt that the establishment of civilized life requires the punishment of wrongdoers and the provision that there should be no statutes of limitations for the greatest atrocities. However, where disbelief reigns, humankind can feel obliged to correct *all* injustice, however remote in time or circumstances. As we know from the past century, such fervor is easily deflected by motives of power and selfishness and can lead to great cruelty and suffering. There arises a sense of "injustice" that is without mercy and becomes indiscriminate, taking no account of human frailty.

Centuries of suffering cannot be overcome by an ambitious humanism that strains to be an earthly substitute for Divine Justice. But from a theological perspective, the incomplete situation gives rise for hope, as the innocent sufferers of injustice can expect that God will in due time bring His own vindication. Faith in a Last Judgment carries the anticipation that there will be an ultimate undoing that finally makes all things right. At the end, all evildoers will lose whatever prestige they had in their own time and stand naked before the Judge. What they counted for in history will now become what they are in truth. [25]

---

good and evil that man does. Someone able to reward the good and punish the bad. No one else but He [sic.] is capable of doing it." *Crossing the Threshold of Hope* (New York: Alfred Knopf, 1994), 183-84). Compare Benedict XVI, *Saved in Hope III*. See also Thiel, *Icons of Hope*, Chapter Four.

25. With respect to the Final Judgment and the reparations of wrongs that it entails, " . . . faith in the Last Judgment is first and foremost hope . . . . I am convinced that questions of justice constitute the essential argument, or in any case the strongest argument in favor of faith in eternal life." *Saved in Hope*. The poem, "The Dream of Gerontius" (1864), by St John Henry Newman, about the dying of an old practicing Catholic, expressed beliefs about the Afterlife that were common to much of Christian England of that time. The poem made reference not only to condemnation or reward after death, but also to a purification of the soul in Purgatory as part of the larger plan of the redemption of men and women. This contrasts well with the Calvinist conception of the damnation of sinners and the Unitarian confidence in universal forgiveness. See John R. Velez, "Newman's Theology in the Dream of Gerontius," *New Blackfriars* 82.967 (2001) 387-98. The *Catechism of the Catholic Church* defines Purgatory as " . . . the final purification of the elect which is entirely different from the punishment of the damned" (Sec. 1031).

Reflections On Old Age

As we reflect in our old age upon these great verities, we begin to see more clearly the relationship between grace and judgment. Grace does not wipe all evil deeds away; indeed, a final accounting is essential to the whole plan of salvation. But if the end were only to be one of absolute justice, it would be fearful for us all. There is within Christianity the countervailing expectation of mercy:

> Thus we find ourselves facing a unique contradiction. On the one hand man needs to have a future beyond death, while on the other hand, he cannot bear the thought. If the promise of a future is to be truly 'hope' or 'redemption' for men, the measure of an eternity must be forgiveness as well. Faith in the future, by which we mean Abraham's faith as fulfilled in Christ, is promise and hope and the true offer of a future only because it provides also a land of forgiveness....[26]

We have the assurance of the Apostle Paul that God has not prepared the terrors of judgment for faithful believers, because for them there is the fullness of salvation in Jesus Christ, whose own cruel death brought our redemption. If we remain faithful to the end, we can go trustfully to meet the Judge who we also know to be our Advocate. Our sinfulness will not cripple us forever, so long as we constantly reach out towards Him who is the source of truth and love. His gaze may be painful in its purification, but it will make us truly ourselves and thus completely of God.[27]

For believers who have been "washed in the blood of the Lamb," Christ is the "door" that opens for us the vision of God and a bliss that has no limits. We try to capture this supreme reality in the expression "eternal life," which is, in some sense, unfortunate, because it may seem to offer a future that is a continuous succession of days in what would constitute a monotonous existence. Better to think of it as a supreme moment of satisfaction for the

---

26. Ratzinger, *Faith and the Future*, 59.

27. "For everyone, life beyond death is connected with the affirmation: 'I believe in the resurrection of the body' and then: I believe in the forgiveness of sins and in life everlasting. This is *Christocentric eschatology*." John Paul II, *Crossing the Threshold of Hope*, 185.

individual person and the whole community of the saved. Together they will be reunited in a banquet of unity where all revenge has given way to forgiveness, where we will be with all who have died in God's Love, and where the fullness of the Lord's peace will forever reign. Faith helps us to move forward towards this transcendent finality by giving new meaning to our unquenchable thirst for perfect happiness.

The Primacy of Faith and Hope

In the philosophies of the Ancient World, the moral status of older persons depended essentially upon the accomplishments, or failures, of their earlier lives. What decisively separated the Christian view of old age from that of these pagan assumptions was the belief in a continuance of moral and spiritual growth during the declining years. In this final period, as well as in the years that preceded it, the struggle between good and evil is a persistent part of our existence. As older persons, unless our personal faculties of reflection and judgment have broken down, what we do each day in terms of justice and mercy will have consequences beyond our dying. So it is that Judgment of the individual person at his or her death and the Final Judgment of the whole of humanity are essential aspects of a Catholic Christianity. But these necessary elements of Christian doctrine must not be allowed to obstruct the peace and joy that are ours through our faith in the Resurrection of Jesus Christ. It is remarkable how little is understood of this supreme reconciliation of heaven and earth.

Authentic faith cannot be an imaginative projection of our desire for happiness. As an infused virtue, it is a disclosure of realities not comprehended by the powers of the mind, something more basic than human knowledge and of greater importance to our personal destinies. But belief does not make mind irrelevant. As Faith grows within us, it is accompanied by thoughtful reflection, even as it leads reason to assent to what it cannot see. Faith also illuminates our understanding through the articulation by the Church of doctrinal statements that capture the basics of

Revelation. But the objective meaning of Christian faith is not limited to dogmatic propositions. More fundamentally, and more personally, faith is a form of trust—an assent to God, who gives us hope and confidence as well as the conviction that He cares for us and for our world.

In his essay in the Symposium *In After Days*, which we have already examined, the Italian historian Guglielmo Ferrero stated, "Man cannot be happy unless he ardently longs for and awaits with assurance, something that he will not be able to obtain while he lives . . . ." This assertion is but half true. Assurance is surely more difficult than longing, but Faith is not just a reaching out towards what is to come after death. It gives us, even now, something of the reality that is eternal, and in doing so draws the future into the present. We should be joyful even now. And we should also realize that our responsibility for the present has an eternal significance.[28]

Jesus Christ is not just someone in whom we believe. He is one with whom we are united in a union that is so close that we see things as He sees them, participating in His view of the world as expressed to us in the Gospels and in the teachings and sacraments of the Church. But all of these great possibilities depend upon our transcending our isolated self-consciousness. The difficulty is that for a long time consciousness has been seen as the paramount source of religious belief; that is, faith is to be found within the identity of the subject who senses the eternal, or, as in the case of Henry James, an inward aesthetic awareness becomes the ultimate ground of being. In contrast, Catholic thought acknowledges an objective reality that comes to us and calls us to both worship and freedom. This requires an openness to something prior to ourselves. As well summarized by Pope Francis:

> Faith's new way of seeing things is centered on Christ. Faith in Christ brings salvation because in him our lives become radically open to a love that precedes us, a love that transforms us from within, acting in us and through us . . . . Faith knows that God has drawn close to us, that Christ has been given to us as a great gift that inwardly

---

28. Benedict XVI, *Saved in Hope*.

transforms us, dwells within us, and thus bestows on us the light that illumines the origin and end of life.[29]

To grasp the full meaning of faith in the Resurrection we must not understand it as leading us to a solitary salvation. We must place ourselves, with all our singularity and uniqueness, in the context of the community of believers. We must also see that our own being is related to the whole of humanity. This sense of wholeness is something that is very difficult for us as Americans to grasp, since our individualistic culture is devoted to placing the separate self at the absolute center of reality.

The New England transcendentalist Ralph Waldo Emerson was a prophet of this particular mode of personal understanding. Emerson strongly believed that each individual had a passion for holiness that empowers him to find the purpose of life within himself. He believed (as did the Unitarians) that the essential truths of Christianity were amenable to individual intuition. In the deepest subjectivity of his self-consciousness, Emerson hoped to build an absolute self that would determine all things for itself. Such a view has its attractiveness, but it is essentially incompatible with Catholic Christianity.[30]

Catholicism is not a private matter. The believer's relationship to God is public as well as interior. The search for holiness may begin in isolation, but it inevitably draws the individual toward others, especially when they realize that it is only in being together with those who share the faith that they all can work out their common aspirations. It is for that reason that Christian faith is ecclesial by its very nature. It rises from the community of believers in the domestic church of the family, to the communal experience of parish life, and then more inclusively to a wider membership in

---

29. *The Light of Faith*, 20.

30. See the analysis of Emerson's ideas in my *Person and Society in American Thought*, Chapter One, "A New England Revival." Archbishop Rowan Williams has said, "The enemy of all proclamation of the Gospel is self-consciousness, and, by definition, we cannot overcome this by being more self-conscious . . . ." *Address to the Thirteenth Ordinary General Assembly of the Synod of Bishops*, Rome, 10 October 2012.

the Universal Church. These interdependencies are all meant to work towards the unity and peace that make up the Mystical Body of Christ.[31]

Christian men and women constitute a "we" but in a way that is not destructive of the distinct person. Admittedly, within the institutional church there is not a celebration of the distinctive personality, and, given its attraction to the multitudes, there is always the danger of its practices imitating the leveling uniformities of mass society. Nevertheless, the unique talents of each individual believer, when put to the service of love, can draw such a particular man or woman to the heights of human spirituality. The cult of canonized Saints testifies to this diversity. How different is Saint Thomas More from Francis of Assisi, or Teresa of Ávila from Saint Maria Goretti? The pursuit of holiness takes great humility, but in the process of sanctification there is no separation of the reality of the individual personality from the demands of the devout life.[32]

The universal call to holiness expressed by the Second Vatican Council broke down the barrier between clergy and laity, as it made clear that both groups are called to pursue spiritual perfection. We need to remember that such a quest applies to the whole span of natural life, including that of old age. The final years are not exempt from the struggle between good and evil, although they also present unique opportunities for spiritual growth.

Throughout the centuries it has been recognized that older men and women can be prone to evils that seem to be an inherent part of aging. The elderly can be, as recounted in *The Canterbury Tales*, filled with "boasting, fibbing, anger and greed." They can turn the virtue of thrift into the vice of miserliness as well as search for solace for their loneliness in bitterness and gossip. Even worse, they can come to lack the confidence and courage to face an unknown future over which they have no control. Some allow the

---

31. Pope Francis, *The Light of Faith*, 22-23. On the ecclesial nature of the family, see John Paul II's Apostolic Exhortation, *The Role of the Christian Family in the Modern World (Familiaris Consortio)*, 1981.

32. "... Christians are 'one' (cf. Gal 3:28), yet in a way that does not make them lose their individuality; in service to others they come into their own in the highest degree ...," in *The Light of Faith*, 22.

prudent carefulness that old age demands to turn into a timidity that takes no risks, even when the good of another is at stake. A more subtle perversion occurs among those who have some faith, however tenuous, in eternal life, but are resigned to doing nothing more in their remaining years than managing the ailments of old age. These unfulfilled persons have convinced themselves that the only happiness is completely beyond this "vale of tears."[33]

It is also unfortunately true that, in our time as well as that of Thoreau, many live lives of "quiet desperation." This malady can afflict men and women of all ages, but does great harm to the elderly. As illnesses and other difficulties multiply, discouragement can turn into despair. With the inexorable increase of all the humiliations and dependencies that "go with the territory," it becomes extremely hard for many older persons to sustain a faith in the possibilities of life; they can, as well, lose all trust in Divine Providence. The situation has many psychological and social causes, but from a moral perspective the problem is that of Sloth, or *Acedia*, one of the traditional capital sins. Such a state does not indicate unwillingness to work, but the refusal by such individuals to strive for fulfillment of their truly human existence. The situation cannot be changed by hectoring admonitions; the only effective therapy is an outreach of love, where one heart speaks with encouraging kindness to another. An affirmation at the deepest levels can make those who suffer from such hopelessness gradually come to believe that it is good that they exist. They may then begin to believe that they can still find some enjoyment in living as well as a greater satisfaction in cultivating an inward spirituality.[34]

All are nourished from within through belief in the Resurrection. In old age a sturdy faith creates many opportunities for individuals to express their love of God and for all brothers and sisters in Christ. Sustained devotion in prayer and worship can purify our intentions, clean us from our faults, and lead us to the heights of contemplation. We show our love for others by expanding the

---

33. John LaFarge, S. J., *Reflections on Growing Old*, Part III.

34. Josef Pieper, "The Obscurity of Hope and Despair," in *Josef Pieper, An Anthology* (San Francisco: Ignatius Press, 1989), Chapter Ten.

breadth and variety of our encounters, always paying special attention to those who suffer.

Interpersonal encounters are closest at hand, and with the right intentions we can close off, as far as possible, all that estranges us from one another and show charity and compassion for those who not only have physical infirmities but also experience the pangs of loneliness. We can show a concern for another's good that runs much deeper than a superficial comradeship, a concern that reaches down into our common destiny. Even in old age, however, the demands of justice and charity extend beyond our immediate surroundings.

In his Encyclical *Charity in Truth*, Pope Benedict XVI pointed out that to love is to desire another person's good, and that this imperative not only applies to immediate relationships but derives also from our membership in a broader society whose common good is "the good of all of us." The opportunities to promote a more inclusive love arise in institutional or political settings; indeed, the love that is shown in these contexts is as meritorious as the charity that is shown in direct interpersonal encounters. The *Emeritus* Pontiff reminds us that we are all called to show this broader love according to our circumstances and the degree of our influence upon the *polis*.[35]

These responsibilities deserve greater attention then they usually receive. While it is obvious that older persons have fewer opportunities for political activity than they might have had in their younger years, such a contraction is no excuse for a total retreat into a private world of family and congenial friends, where from such comfortable surroundings one can simply denounce everything that happens in the public world. Nor is it sufficient simply to show an interest in programs and policies that affect the social or financial interests of senior citizens. Older persons living in this twenty-first century should show that magnanimity and mature sense of justice so well described by Dante.

Even as our opportunities for action are limited, we can still do many things to promote the common good of our broader

---

35. *Charity in Truth*, Introduction, 7.

societies so long as we see them as objects of our love and concern. With our wisdom and experience we can do much more than we may realize to create a more humane society. Even as our physical powers decline, most have sufficient energy to communicate with relevant media outlets and express a balanced and well-thought out opinion on matters of general importance. We can keep in touch with our representatives in the state or federal government. We can also participate in public conversations about the pressing issues of our time and bring to such discussions a clarity and spirit of reconciliation for which there is a great need in our deeply divided politics. When animated by a love for all with whom we share a common life, and when not driven by ideological compulsions, the pursuit of a common good is an act of charity that is of great importance to the task of bringing the Kingdom of God down to earth.[36]

One of the mysteries of old age is that all the losses that we experience create the opportunity for the one great and sustaining Hope to arise. Through it we gain the expectation of a personal immortality, and an entirely new life of unity and peace. Thus there arises an experience unique to the advanced years: the dialectic of an unavoidable decline that is resisted by a great expectation. We are enabled in our weakness to do things that are of eternal importance, even in simple situations, and we are sustained even in our gravest moments by the love of the Creator and Redeemer of our lives.

In this awaiting upon God through service to others there is an unveiling of the full significance of the Resurrection:

> For life is ultimately a process of deification, a gradual transformation of every human soul by the Spirit. We must come to understand that we are taken up into this movement and try to live in accordance with it, to realize that each of us is united to all others, who are themselves taken up, and that we are striving toward a particular goal. In this our lives are enlightened and find their meaning.[37]

---

36. See Tournier, *Learn To Grow Old*, II.

37. Jean Danielou, *Prayer, The Mission of the Church* (Grand Rapids: Eerdmans, 1996) 50.

Bibliography

Alden, H. M. "The Other Side of Mortality." In *In After Days or Thoughts on the Future Life*. New York: Harper, 1910.
Alighieri, Dante. *The Divine Comedy*.
———. *The Banquet (Convivio)*.
Aristotle. *The Rhetoric in the Basic Works of Aristotle*. Edited by Richard McKeon. New York: Random House, 1941.
Arnold, Matthew. *Selected Poems and Prose*. Everyman's Library, 1985.
Auden, W. H. *Selected Poems*. Edited by Edward Mendelson. London: Faber & Faber, 1979.
Bacon, Francis. "Of Youth and Age." In *The Essays of Francis Bacon*. New York: Peter Pauper, 2008.
Bacon, Friar Roger. *His Discoveries of the Miracles of Art, Nature and Magick*. Translated by T.M. London: Simon Miller, 1659.
Barnes, Julian. *Nothing to be Afraid Of*. New York: Alfred Knopf, 2008.
Bellamy, Edward. *Looking Backward: 2000-1887*. New York: Random House, 1951.
Benedict XVI. *Encyclical Letter, Saved in Hope*. Spe. Salvi, 2007.
———. "Address to the Elderly in Care." In *The Tablet*. February 16, 2013.
Beyond Therapy: Biotechnology and the Pursuit of Happiness. A Report of the President's Council on Bioethics. Washington, D.C.: Dana Press, 2003.
Brown, Ivor. *Shaw in His Time*. 1965.
Carter, Jimmy. *The Virtues of Aging*. New York: Ballantine, 1998.
Catechism of the Catholic Church. 2nd edition. United States Catholic Conference, 1994.
Channing, William Ellery. "The Moral Argument Against Calvinism." In *The Works of William Ellery Channing*. Boston: The American Unitarian Association, 1975.
Chase, Karen. *The Victorians and Old Age*. Oxford: Oxford University Press, 2009.
Chesterton, G. K. *Chaucer*. New York: Sheed & Ward, 1956.
Chittister, Joan. *The Gift of Years: Growing Old Gracefully*. New York: Blue Ridge, 2008.
Cicero. *On Old Age (De Senectute)*. In *Cicero Selected Works*, translated by Michael Grant. Baltimore: Penguin, 1960.
Commager, Henry Steele. *Theodore Parker*. Boston: Beacon, 1947.

Bibliography

Cornaro, Luigi. *The Art of Living Long.* Milwaukee, WI: William F. Butler, 1916.

Covey, Herbert. "Old Age Portrayed by the Ages of Life: Models from the Middle Ages to the 16th Century." In *The Gerontologist* 5 (1989).

Danielou, Jean. *Prayer: The Mission of the Church.* Grand Rapids: Eerdmans, 1996.

De Beauvoir, Simone. *The Coming of Age.* Translated by Patrick O'Brian. New York: G. P. Putnam, 1992.

De Montaigne, Michel. *Essais.* New York: Heritage, 1988.

De Rapp, Robert. *Man Against Aging.* New York: St. Martins, 1960.

Demos. "Old Age in Early New England." In *The American Journal of Sociology* (1978).

Emerson, Ralph Waldo. "Society and Solitude." In *The Works of Ralph Waldo Emerson, Volume 2.* Boston: Fireside, 1909.

Epicurus. *The Art of Happiness.* New York: Penguin, 2012.

Ferrero, Guglielmo. "The Life after This." In *After Days.*

Fischer, David Hackett. *Growing Old in America.* Oxford: Oxford University Press, 1976.

Fischer, Irving. *Report on National Vitality.* (1909).

Francis, Pope. *The Light of Faith.* Encyclical Letter (2013).

Hall, Donald. "Out the Window: The View in Winter." *The New Yorker.* January 20, 2012.

Hall, F. Stanley. *Senescence: The Last Half of Life.* New York: D. Appleton, 1922.

Hayes, Maria S. "The Supposed Golden Age for the Aged in Ancient Rome." In *The Gerontologist* 11 (1963).

Holmes, Oliver Wendell. *The Autocrat of the Breakfast Table (1882) Common Reader.* 2001.

Horace, *Odes.*

Howells, William Dean. "A Counsel of Consolation." In *In After Days or Thoughts on the Future Life.* New York: Harper, 1910.

Innocent III, Pope. "The Misery of Man (*De Contempto Mundi*)." In *Two Views of Man,* translated by Giannozzo Manetti. New York: Frederick Unger, 1966.

Jacoby, Susan. *Never Say Die: The Myth and Marketing of the New Old Age.* New York: Pantheon, 2011.

James, Henry. "Is there Life After Death." In *In After Days or Thoughts on the Future Life.* New York: Harper, 1910.

James, William. *The Will to Believe and Other Essays in Popular Philosphy (1909).* New York: Dover, 1959.

John Paul II. *Crossing the Threshold of Faith.* New York: Alfred Knopf, 1994.

———. *Letter to the Elderly,* 1999.

———. *The Role of the Christian Family in the Modern World (Familiaris Consortio),* 1981.

Jung, C. G. *Modern Man in Search of a Soul.* New York: Harcourt Brace & World, 1933.

BIBLIOGRAPHY

Kant, Emmanuel. *Critique of Pure Reason*. Translated by N. K. Smith. New York: St. Martin's, 1965.

Kebric, Robert. "Aging in Pliny's Letters: A View from the Second Century, A.D." In *the Gerontologist* 5 (1989).

Kinsella, Kevin, and Wan He. *An Aging World*. Washington, D.C: Census Bureau, 2009.

La Farge, John. *Reflections on Growing Old*. New York: America, 1963.

Lawler, Peter. "The Care-Giving Society." *The New Atlantis*. 2005.

Lepore, Jill. "Twilight, Growing Old and Even Older." *The New Yorker*. March 4, 2011.

Lewis, C. S. *The Four Loves*. Glasgow, Scotland: William Collins, 1960.

Mann, Charles C. "The Coming Death Shortage." *The Atlantic Monthly*. May 2005.

Mann, Thomas. "Introduction." In *The Goethe Treasury Selected Prose and Poetry*. Mineola, NY: Dover, 2006.

Maritain, Jacques. *The Degrees of Knowledge*. Translated by Gerald B. Phelan. South Bend, IN: University of Notre Dame Press, 1995.

———. *Creative Intuition in Art and Poetry*. New York: Meridian, 1955.

Meilander, Gilbert. "Thinking about Aging." *First Things*. April 2011.

Metchnickoff, Elie. *Th eNature of Man: Stuides in Optimistic Philosophy*. 1905.

More, Thomas. *Utopia*. Translated by Paul Turner. London: Penguin, 1965.

Morgan, Margery M. "Back to Methusula, The Poet and The City." In *G.B. Shaw: A Collection of Critical Essays*, edited by R. J. Kaufmann. Englewood Cliffs, NJ: Prentiss Hall, 1965.

Morris, William. *New from Nowhere*. Boston: Roberts Brothers, 1890.

Motto, Lydia. "Seneca on Old Age." *Estudios Latinos*. 2000.

Murphy, Cornelius. *Person and Society in American Thought*. New York: Peter Lang, 2007.

Nagel, Thomas. "After You're Gone." *New York Review of Books*. January 9, 2014.

Newman, John Henry. *The Dream of Gerontius*. Staten, NY: St. Paul/Alba House, 2001.

Nuland, Sherwin B. *The Gift of Aging*. New York: Random House, 2007.

Osler, William. "The Fixed Period." *Archives of Internainoal Medicine* 161.2.

The Pastoral Constitution on the Church in the Modern World, Intoructionary Statement. In *The Documents of Vatican II*, edited by Walter Abbott. New York: America, 1966.

Pieper, Josef. *Leisure, The Basis of Culture*. South Bend, IN: St. Augustine, 1998.

———. "The Obscurity of Hope and Despair." In *Josef Pieper, An Anthology*. San Francisco: Ignatius, 1998.

Plato. *The Republic*. New York: Penguin, 1998.

Ratzinger, Joseph. *Faith and the Future*. San Francisco: Ignatius, 2007.

Roth, Philip. *Everyman*. Boston: Houghton Mifflin, 2006.

Russell, Bertrand. *In Praise of Idleness and Other Essays*. London: George Allen, 1935.

BIBLIOGRAPHY

Sacred Congregation for the Doctrine of the Faith. "Letter Concerning Certain Questions of Eschatology." 1979.

Secunda, Victoria. *By Youth Possessed: The Denial of Age in America*. Indianapolis: Bobbs-Merrill, 1984.

Shakespeare, William. *As You Like It*. 1623.

Shaler, Nathaniel S. *The Individual: A Study of Life and Death*. New York: D. A. Appleton, 1902.

Shulamith, Shahar. *Growing Old in the Middle Ages*. Translated by Youl Lotan. London: Routledge, 1997.

Shaw, Bernard. *Back to Methuselah: A Metabiological Pontatcich*. Oxford: Oxford University Press, 1947.

Simpson, Alan, and Erskine Bowles. *Report of the National Committee on Fiscal Responsibiliity and Reform*. December 1, 2010.

Souvestre, Emile. *The Pleasures of Old Age*. 1868.

Stearns, Peter. "The Obsolescence of Old Age in America 1865–1914." *Journal of Social History* 8.1 (1974).

Stuart, Christopher. "Is There Life After Death? Henry James' Response to the New York Edition." *Colby Quarterly* 35.2 (1999).

Strauch. "The Date of Emerson's *Terminus*." *PMLA* 64.4 (1950).

Tennyson, Lord Alfred. "Ulysses." In *Selected Poems*. New York: Penguin Classics, 2007.

Thiel, John E. *Icons of Hope, The Last Things in Catholic Imagination*. Notre Dame, IN: University of Notre Dame Press, 2013.

Thomson, William Hanna. "The Future State." In *In After Days*. 1910.

Thoreau, Henry David. *Walden*. 1854.

Tournier, Paul. *Learning to Grow Old*. Louisville, KY: Westminster John Knox, 1972.

Trollope, Anthony. *The Fixed Period*. 1862. New York: Penguin, 1993.

United Nations General Assembly Res. 46/91.16. December, 1991.

Velez, John. "Newman's Theology in the Dream of Gerontius." In *New Blackfriars* 82 (2001).

Vienna Internaional Plan on Aging. New York: United Nations, 1983.

Williams, Rowan. *Address to the Thirteenth Ordinary General Assembly of the Synod of Bishops*. October 10, 2012.

Index

Absolute Self, 109
Abrahamic tradition, 98, 106
Acedia: See Sloth
Accountability at death, 101
Adams, John, 25
Adenauer, Konrad, 41
Adultos Mejores, 46
Advanced senescence, 54
Aesthetic delights: See Beauty
Aesthetic consciousness, 99
After Life, 94, 100
Age Segregation, 81
Alden, Henry Mills, 96
Alighieri, Dante: See Dante
Alzheimer's disease, 43
America: circumstances of the elderly in, xi
Aquinas: on honoring the elderly, 13
Aristotle: on old age, 2–3
Arnold, Matthew, 19, 44, 61
Artistic consciousness, 98–99
Auden, 55
Augustine, Saint, 13
Average life span, 31, 46

Bacon, Roger, 13–14
Bacon, Sir Francis, 16
Barnes, Julian, 86
Beauty: nature of, 79
Benedict XVI, Pope: on old age, 56; on pursuit of the common good, 112
Bereavement, 94
Body: nature of, 42; care of, 53
Bradstreet, Anne, 23

Browning, Robert, 19, 66
Buber, Martin, 56

Catholicism: its nature, 109–110
Centenarians, 54
Cephalus, 2
Channing, William Ellery, 94
Chaucer, x, 14
Childhood: as distinct phase of life, 29
Chinese Civilization, 1
Christian Faith: 109–112
Churchill, Sir Winston, 40
Cicero: on Old Age, 3–6; on death, 30, 58, 89–90
Common Good: pursuit of as act of charity, 113
Compression of morbidity, 53
Conscience: as site of personal identity, 81
Consumer culture, 30
Conversation Salons, 75–76
Council of Elders, 41
Council on Bioethics: Report on Biotechnology, 43–45

Dante: on the ages of man, 9; on a noble old age, 10–11; on final happiness, 91
Darwinian principles, 88
De Montaigne, Michel: on development of the human soul, 15, 63, 74; on death, 89

Index

Death: complex nature of, 100; and proximity of judgment, 18, 102
Deification, 113
Dementia, 71
Democracy: principles of, 24, 41
Democratic age, 74
Dialogue: Between older persons and other adults, 51–52
Divine Grace, 102–103
Divine Mercy, 104
Divine Providence, 85, 111

Edwards. Jonathan, 92
Electronic Media, 77
Emerson, Ralph Waldo: opinions on old age, xi, 24–26, 61, 74; on Christianity, 109
Enlightenment, 89,
Epicurus, 90
Eternal life: ambiguity of expression, 106; as banquet of unity, 107
Everyman, 87–88

Faith: its nature, 107–109; communal quality, 109; as present reality, 108
Ferrero, Guglielmo, 97, 107, 108
Final Judgment: See Last Judgment
First World War, 39
Francis, Pope, 109–110
Franklin, Benjamin, 25
Friendship: importance of in old age, 83–84

Galen, 12
Gender Differences, 82
Generations: distance between, 17, 47; conversations between, 49–51
Gerontology, 53
Genetics, 42–43
Goethe, Johan, x, 16–17, 70
God as a person, 95

Good and evil: struggle between, 101, 107, 110
Gun Control, 76

Hall, G.Stanley: Theories of old age, 33–36; on marriage and longevity, 37, 81
Happiness: in after life, 98, 106; as solitary fulfillment, 81; in extensive relationships, 81 Dante's understanding of, 91; in human maturity, 86
Harper's Bazaar, 92
Hebrew Scriptures, 22, 61
Holmes, Oliver Wendell: on the stages of life, xi, 27–28, 62; on old age as a disease, 41
Hope: as expectation of personal immortality, 113
Horace, 3, 12
Howe, Julia Ward, xvi, 92, 95
Howells, William Dean, xvi, 92, 93
Human Being: completeness of, xvi; final destiny, 110–113
Human Relatedness: horizontal and vertical aspects, 80–85

Immaturities, 51
Immortality: expectation of, 92
In After Days: Thoughts On The Future Life, 93, 101
Individual Personality: development after death, 97, 110
Individualistic culture, 109
Injustice: sense of, 105
Innocent III, Pope: treatise on old age, 12–13
Institutional care, x, 18,
Intellectual life, 73
Interpersonal encounters, 82–85

James, Henry: on after life, xvi, 92, 98; on artistic consciousness, 99–101

Index

James, William, 101
Jesus Christ: words of, 95; return of, 104; union with, 108
John xxiii, Pope: and Second Vatican Council, 41
Johnson, Samuel: on intergenerational relations, x, 16–17, 60;on retirement, 18; on preparation for death, 18
Jordan, Elizabeth Gardner, 92
Jung, 70
Juvenal, 3

Kantian principles, 103
Kass Report: See Council on Bioethics

Last Judgment: as correction of historical injustice, 104; in Scripture and art, 102; relation to Faith and Hope, 105–106
Laughter, 85
Leisure: nature of, xiv, 72–73
Life expectancy, 30–31
Longevity, 31–58,
Longfellow, 26–27,
Love: as an attribute of personality, 95; inclusive quality of, 112

MacArthur, Douglas: career longevity, 41
Magnanimity of older persons, 10–11, 79
Mandela, Nelson: on creation of Council of Elders, 41
Marriage and old age, 37, 81
Mass Media, 72,
Mass mentality, 74
Massachusetts Bay Colony, 61
Mather, Cotton, 22
Maximum life-span, 46
Medieval practices, 91

Men: gatherings of in old age, xv, 83
Metchinikoff, Elie, 39
Middle Age, 52
Middle Ages, 8–11, 59
Modern Man: and explanations of existence, 89
Montaigne, Michel: See de Montaigne
More, Thomas, 14
Morris, William, 20–21
Mortality: value of, 96

New England Calvinism, 92
New England Renaissance, xi, 24–28
Newman, John Henry, Cardinal, 28, 62, 68
Neurological Research, 72
Nirvana of Buddhism, 99

Old Age: Advanced stages of, 53–57; nature of, 42, 58, relationships in, 80–85; Vices of, 1–5, 78, 110
Older persons: basic entitlements of, 46; employment of, 49; on death and dying, 89; challenged to magnanimity, 112 isolation of, 46
Oliphant, Margaret, 20
Osler, William, 29

Parker, Theodore, 95
Paul, Saint, 42, 85, 106
Personal existence, 98, 110
Personal identity, 68–73
Personal immortality, 94–97, 103–104
Phelps, Elizabeth Stuart, 93–95
Plato: on old age, ix, 1–3
Platonists, 90
Pliny the younger, 6–7
Prayer, 85–86
Predestination, xvii, 92, 94
Purgatory, 112

Index

Puritanism, 22, 91–92, 94

Redemption, 91
Reflection, 80
Relationships: for civilized democracy, 80; interpersonal, 81; with God, 85
Report On National Vitality, 31, 38, 48
Retirement Communities, 47
Resurrection of Jesus Christ, 104
Roncalli, Angelo, See John xxiii
Roth, Philip, 87
Roosevelt, Theodore, 31, 97
Russell, Bertrand, 74

Saint Francis of Assisi, 110
Saint Maria Goretti, 110
Saint Theresa of Avila, 110
Saint Thomas More, 110
Science and Technology, 41–45
Second Coming, 104
Self-Consciousness: artistic quality, 99–100; moral dimensions, 101
Self Identities, 67, 80, 109
Seneca, 7–8
Senility, 71
Senior Citizens, 69
Shakespeare: on infirmities of old age, x, 15, 60
Shaler, Nathaniel: longevity in animals and humans compared,

Shaw, George Bernard: drama on longevity, 39–40
Simpson, Alan: *National Commission on Fiscal Responsibility and Reform*, 41, 77
Souvestre, Emile, on the pleasures of old age, 21–22
Symposium on The After Life, 16, 92–101

Temperance, 69
Television: effects on the elderly, 71
Tennyson, 70
Thoreau, 24, 111
Transcendentals of comprehension, 71
Trollope, Anthony, 19, 61
Twentieth Century, 65
Unadultness, 51,
Unitarianism, 94
United Nations General Assembly: on rights of older persons, 48–49
Universal Call to Holiness, 110

Very-Old: plight of, xiii, 53–57
'Vale of Tears' 110

Will, purpose of, 70
Women in Old Age, xv, 82
Wisdom of the Elderly, 75–76

www.ingramcontent.com/pod-product-compliance
Lightning Source LLC
Chambersburg PA
CBHW050830160426
43192CB00010B/1970